DISCOVERING THE VILLAGES
OF FRANCE

DISCOVERING
THE VILLAGES OF
F·R·A·N·C·E

Michael Busselle

BCA
LONDON · NEW YORK · SYDNEY · TORONTO

Illustrated opposite:
A fortified gateway leading into the small hilltop village of
Montréal, which overlooks the valley of the Serein.

Illustrated on page 1:
An ancient fountain in Peillon.
Illustrated on page 2:
A pollarded plane tree decorates the front of a village house in
Hautefort.

This edition published 1991 by BCA
by arrangement with Pavilion Books Limited,
196 Shaftesbury Avenue, London WC2H 2JL

CN 8620

Text and Photographs © Mike Busselle 1991

Designed by Andrew Barron & Collis Clements Associates

Printed and bound in Italy by L.E.G.O.

10   9   8   7   6   5   4   3   2   1

CONTENTS

INTRODUCTION

I have just a hazy memory of my 'first' French village, chanced upon thirty or so years ago during a motoring holiday. I know only that it was somewhere in south-west France, set on a hill, and had a steep cobbled main street. I don't remember its name and I have been unable to identify it since. Anyway, it was at that moment my addiction began. Always an avid reader of guide-books and a devout 'mapophile', on subsequent visits to France I would always seek out an interesting village or two on my route. It became a sort of hobby.

This book stemmed from a desire to put the villages I had already visited into a semblance of order and to have an excuse to explore all of the others I had read or heard about. It turned out to be something of a marathon task. I travelled over 50,000 kilometres and visited more than a thousand villages to arrive at those included in the book.

The criteria for inclusion were rather subjective. Sometimes a village gave me a little lift of the spirits when I first entered it. On other occasions there would be a more gradual appreciation of its setting or atmosphere. Generally it was the overall impression of a place which tended to influence my choice rather than its history or the possession of a single significant feature.

Some of the villages do have fine churches or castles – Vézelay, Conques or Najac, for instance – and are well known; some, like Montferrand-du-Périgord or Frespech, have no particularly outstanding architectural features and are just pretty and appealing; while others, like Bigorre or Ste-Croix-en-Jarez, are secretive and remote. With just a couple of exceptions, the villages included have a population of less than a thousand, and many are tiny communities of only a hundred or so people.

The villages are arranged in groups, so that a sequence can be visited in the form of a tour. Alternatively, you can just dip into the book and visit places which are close to a chosen route or convenient for an excursion from a holiday base. Either way, the large-scale Michelin maps are absolutely essential for finding your way to these and other marvellous villages – and there are thousands more to discover – as many of them are not marked on smaller-scale maps. I wish you happy hunting!

Michael Busselle, 1991

A butcher's shop sign (opposite) in the Alsatian village of Soultzbach-les-Bains in the Munster valley. (Above) Two elderly ladies take a rest from sweeping the courtyard of their farmhouse in the village of Hunspach.

CHAPTER ONE
NORTH-WEST FRANCE

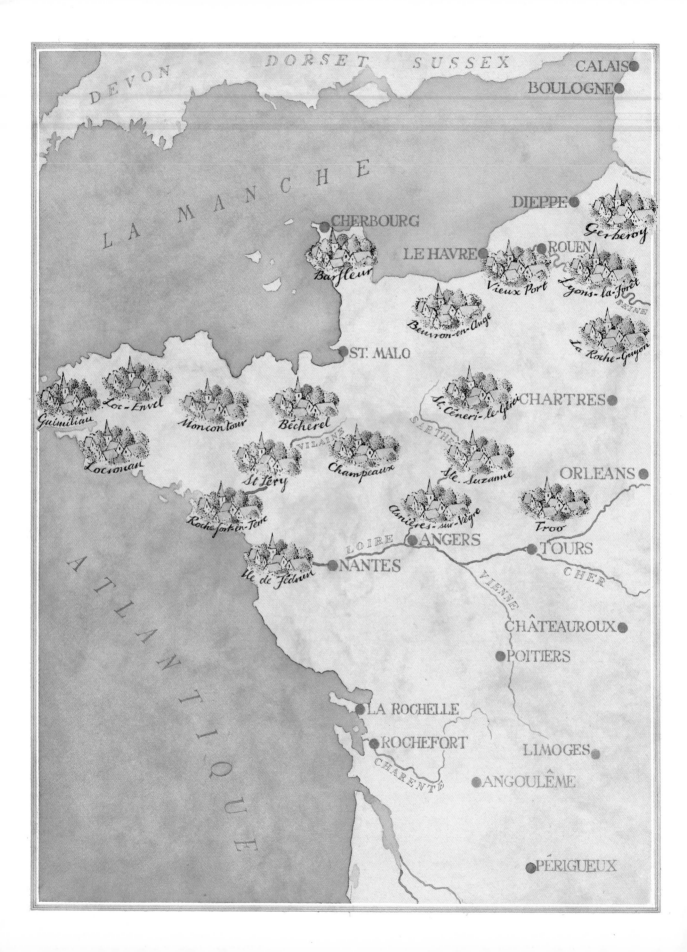

DEVON   DORSET   SUSSEX

CALAIS
BOULOGNE

LA MANCHE

CHERBOURG

DIEPPE

Gerberoy

LE HAVRE   ROUEN

Barfleur

Vieux Port   *Lyons-la-Forêt*

SEINE

Beuvron-en-Auge

La Roche-Guyon

ST. MALO

St. Cénéri-le-Gérei   CHARTRES

Loc-Envel

Guimiliau   *Moncontour*   *Bécherel*

SARTHE

Locronan   VILAINE   *Champeaux*   *Ste. Suzanne*   ORLEANS

St. Léry

Asnières-sur-Vègre   *Troo*

Rochefort-in-Terre

LOIRE   ANGERS   TOURS

Île de Fédrun   NANTES   CHER

ATLANTIQUE

VIENNE

CHÂTEAUROUX

POITIERS

LA ROCHELLE

ROCHEFORT   LIMOGES

CHARENTE   ANGOULÊME

PÉRIGUEUX

GERBEROY · LYONS-LA-FORÊT
LA ROCHE-GUYON · VIEUX-PORT

Inland from the channel port of Dieppe is a countryside known as the Pays de Bray. It is a peaceful rural backwater of low hills and shallow valleys lying between the chalky downlands of the Pays de Caux in Normandy and the Picardy plateau. Predominantly dairy country, the landscape is one of green meadows outlined by hedgerows and thickets.

Gerberoy

On the south-eastern edge of this region, about 25km north-west of Beauvais, almost on the border between Picardy and Normandy, lies the village of *Gerberoy*. It is built on the crest of a hill overlooking open farmland near Songeons.

Gerberoy is tiny and has the sort of unreal prettiness which is associated with chocolate boxes and Victorian watercolours. Its charm, however, seems quite uncontrived, and the village gives the impression that it is surprised by the admiration it attracts.

Within the remains of ancient ramparts, the main street winds up a gentle hill. It is lined with terraced houses patterned with wooden beams and brickwork reflecting the architectural styles of both Picardy and Normandy. In summer the houses are draped with old-fashioned climbing roses with the colours of faded, hand-tinted photographs. A festival of roses is held in the village on the third Sunday in June.

The main street leads to a small square where there is a covered market hall and a well. On each side there are narrow streets with ancient timbered cottages. One lane leads up to a sixteenth-century church set on a knoll above the village. On the way to it you pass through a stone arch, once the entrance to a fortress.

The village dates from 922 when Vicomte Fulco built a castle there. At the end of the twelfth century, after several battles

A traditional house in the postcard-pretty village of Gerberoy on the borders of Picardy and Normandy. (Previous page) The old houses and fortified church of Barfleur seen from the rock-strewn edge of its sheltered harbour.

with the English, the village was fortified by ramparts. Since then it has seen conflict with, among others, William the Conqueror (who was wounded here) and the Dukes of Burgundy. Its name is derived from the word *gerbe*, meaning sheaf. During the Revolution the community was ignominiously obliged to change its name to Gerbe-le-Montagne. Later the population declined, but the village was revitalized in the first part of this century when a group of artists led by Henri de Sidaner made it their home.

There is no hotel in Gerberoy, but there are a number of *chambres d'hôte* and *Gîtes* available in the vicinity. There is a café-restaurant, the Hostellerie de Vieux Logis, and a small museum of local history in the town hall.

Gastronomically this region shares the cuisine of both Picardy and Normandy. Neufchâtel-en-Bray (where there is a lively country market on Saturdays) is known for its cylindrical creamy cow's-milk cheese called Bondon. Coeur de Bray is a similar cheese made in a heart-shaped mould. Another great cheese of the region is the pungent creamy Maroilles from the Aisne.

To the north of Gerberoy is the old spa town of Forges-les-Eaux, popularized in the seventeenth century by Louis XIII and Cardinal Richelieu. There is a museum of horse-drawn carriages in the park and a ceramics museum in the town hall. At St-Germer-de-Fly, to the south-west, is a huge Gothic abbey church and chapel with fine stone figures and a rose window.

Lyons-la-Forêt

South-west of Gerberoy lies the Forêt de Lyons, a magnificent beech forest where the Dukes of Normandy once hunted. On a rise in the centre of the woods is the village of Lyons-la-Forêt. While Gerberoy is rather retiring, Lyons-la-Forêt is a lively village with good shops, restaurants and hotels. It's close enough to Paris to be a popular centre for weekend cottagers. The patron of a small café on the square told me that the permanent population of about 250 rises to nearer 800 at weekends.

Fine timber-framed houses surround a triangular cobbled square, in the centre of which is a covered market hall with an exceptional eighteenth-century timbered roof. It is still used for the weekly market on Saturdays.

The village originated with a château built in the twelfth century by the English King Henry I, who died here in 1135. Many of the houses have very grand façades dating from the seventeenth and eighteenth centuries. It was in one of these houses that Maurice Ravel composed *Le Tombeau de Couperin*. The twelfth-century church of St Denis close by has a timber belfry and some fine wooden carvings in the nave.

To the north-west of Lyons-la-Forêt is the attractive village of Ry, built on the banks of the River Crevon. It is reputed to be the setting for Gustave Flaubert's novel *Madame*

An old timbered house overlooking the square of La Ferrière-sur-Risle, in the centre of which is a large covered market hall. (Opposite) One of the arches of the covered market hall in the village of Gerberoy.

Bovary, and a monument to the author has been erected in the village centre. In an ancient cider house on the river bank is a museum of mechanical models, many of which represent scenes from the novel. There is also a reconstruction of a chemist's shop owned by one of the novel's main characters, M. Homais.

The neighbouring village of Vascoeuil is famous for its château, which dates from the fourteenth century. In the gardens are reconstructions of traditional thatched Normandy cottages, and the courtyard has a fine seventeenth-century dovecot together with carvings and mosaics by a number of famous artists including Braque and Dali. There is a lovely sixteenth-century manor house in the tiny village of Heronchelles, set attractively in a small wooded valley a few kilometres to the north.

La Roche-Guyon

Heading south from Lyons-la-Forêt you pass through the countryside of the Vexin on the way to the Seine. Here it is a broad busy river, making its way in a series of looping curves towards Rouen and its estuary at Le Havre. *La Roche-Guyon* is a small village on the north bank. There is a fine tree-shaded promenade along the riverside with park benches where you can sit and watch the big ships and barges pass by.

The village dates from the twelfth century, and the remains of a feudal castle from that period still sit above the village on top of a chalk cliff which is tunnelled by ancient caves. Below the cliff is a château with grand stables flanking a wide courtyard. It was built first in the thirteenth century and altered in the eighteenth. It suffered bomb damage in 1944 (it was used as Rommel's headquarters during the Normandy battles) and was extensively restored after the war.

The domain of La Roche-Guyon has been in the possession of various noble families through the centuries and was a favourite place of painters and poets like Victor Hugo and Claude Monet. In the village is a fifteenth-century church, a carved stone fountain and an eighteenth-century market, now the town hall. There are two hotel-restaurants in the village, Le St-Georges and Le Vieux Donjon, and a restaurant called Le Vieux Logis.

Upstream from here is Vétheuil, for a few years Monet's home and frequent inspiration. A short distance downstream, a small road leads up on to the *corniche*, a wooded hillside from which there are superb views of the Seine.

Further downstream is Giverny. On the edge of what is a rather nondescript village are Monet's house and gardens, which create a breathtakingly beautiful blend of colours at most times of the year. Now a museum on a grand scale, the house, with its faithfully preserved interior, the gardens which he designed and the famous lily ponds (reached by a tunnel under the road) evoke the mood and quality of his paintings in an almost uncanny way.

To the west of Giverny, beyond Evreux and Conches-en-Ouche, is the valley of the Risle, a tributary of the Seine. La Ferrière-sur-Risle, on the D140, is a very charming little village with a large square surrounded by timbered houses. In the centre is a fourteenth-century covered market, sadly now used for car parking. A nice old church, also dating from the fourteenth century, peeps over the rooftops. It has a fine oak altar-piece and several polychrome statues. There are several shops, a café and also a small hotel.

Vieux-Port

The Risle joins the Seine north-west of Pont Audemer, below the Tancarville bridge, the last point at which the river can be crossed and an impressive piece of civil engineering. To the east and south of the river is the Parc Régional de Brotonne., a dense growth of pine, beech and oak trees covering nearly 100,000 acres. A number of routes lead through the park, revealing many aspects of the traditional ways of Normandy life.

There is a *route des chaumières*, which traces the most picturesque of the thatched farms and cottages, and a route leading through the orchards, where you can see the luxuriant blossom in springtime and buy fruit from the farms in autumn. There are a number of villages where traditional crafts can be seen, a bread oven and a sabot maker at La Haye-de-Routot, for example, an apple house and forge at Ste-Opportune-la-Mare, and a stone mill at Hauville.

The Marais Vernier, just south of the Tancarville bridge, is a fascinating region where ancient timbered farms and cottages are hidden among apple orchards. A road leads along the edge of the dike (which was built in the sixteenth century by Dutch engineers), with fine views across the drained and reclaimed lowlands which border the Seine estuary.

Between the forest and the *marais* lies the tiny village of Vieux-Port, strung out along the river bank. Here some of the prettiest timber-framed cottages and thatched houses of the region look out over the river.

The imposing courtyard and stables frame the château of La Roche-Guyon on the banks of the Seine.

Here I spoke to an elderly man who was a retired ship's captain and had bought a house beside the Seine so that he could watch the big ships pass by from his window. No shops, hotel or even a bar that I could see – just a small church and tranquillity.

A few broad loops upstream towards Rouen, in a very beautiful setting below steep cliffs, is the riverside village of La Bouille. In complete contrast to Vieux-Port, this village has a number of good hotels and restaurants with rooms and terraces overlooking the river. Hôtel St-Pierre has comfortable modern rooms with good river views, and the excellent cuisine has earned it a *Michelin* rosette.

Downstream, at the widest part of the Seine estuary, is the enchanting port of Honfleur. Although it is now a largish town, the centre of Honfleur is as compact and self-contained as any village and, in spite of its immense popularity, quite unspoilt. One of the most delightful country markets in France takes place here each Saturday in the cobbled square round the wooden Norman church.

*Everyone's dream of a Normandy cottage set on the banks
of the Seine in the peaceful village of Vieux-Port.
(Opposite) Timbered houses line the street leading to the
small market hall of Lyons-la-Forêt.*

BEUVRON-EN-AUGE · ST-CÉNERI-LE-GÉREI
STE SUZANNE · ASNIÈRES-SUR-VÈGRE · TROO

To the south of Honfleur is the country-side of the Auge. This is quintessential Normandy, a land of apples and cream, cider and cheese, orchards and manor houses, timbered farms and thatched cottages. In the heart of this welcoming landscape is the small village of Beuvron-en-Auge, set beside the River Doigt.

Beuvron-en-Auge

It is little more than a single street which opens out into a small square in the centre of which is a covered market. At the entrance of the village is the manor of Le Logis, a grand house dating from the sixteenth century with intricately patterned timbering ornamented by wooden sculptures.

Many of the houses date from the six-teenth and seventeenth centuries, but the village had its origins in the twelfth. Its name refers to a place where beavers swim. During the Hundred Years War the community was seized by the family of d'Harcourt, who built a château and established it as the stronghold of the region. The château and its fortifica-tions were dismantled at the time of the Revolution and only the timber-framed houses were allowed to remain.

There are no hotels in Beuvron, but there are several *gîtes ruraux* in the area. The village has three restaurants, La Boule d'Or, La Galère and La Pave d'Auge. The latter is housed in the former covered market hall and its proprietor, Mme Engel, offers a cuisine which has been rewarded by a *Michelin* rosette.

On the second Sunday in May a gera-nium fair is held, and the third Sunday in November is the day of the cider fair.

The village is on the official cider route, a product – taken very seriously in these parts – which is made, bottled, tasted and sold in much the same way as a good wine. Calvados is a brandy distilled from cider and aged in

The medieval hump-back bridge of Asnières-sur-Vègre spans a peaceful river. (Previous page) The picturesque old port of Honfleur surrounded by its distinctive tall narrow houses has changed little over the years.

oak casks, and Pommeau an aperitif made by adding cider 'must' to Calvados. The village bakery, during my visit, offered both apple and cider bread.

Cider is also an ingredient in many dishes. The classic *tripes à la mode de Caen*, for example, is made by simmering tripe and vegetables in cider spiked with calvados. *Sauce Normande*, served with fish and white meat dishes, is made by combining the region's thick yellow cream with cider and egg yolks. *Poulet vallée d'auge* is chicken cooked in a sauce of cream and madeira thickened with egg yolks.

Camembert and the creamy yellow cheese of neighbouring Pont l'Evêque are perhaps the best-known of the region. Pavé d'Auge is similar in taste and texture to the latter, and Livarot is a stronger and more pungent variant.

A few kilometres to the south is the village of Crèvecoeur-en-Auge, where there is an eleventh-century fortified manor, now restored, which houses the Schlumberger Museum, devoted to the history of petroleum research. The neighbouring village of Clermont-en-Auge has a small chapel from which there is fine panorama over the Auge countryside. To the north-east is Beaumont-en-Auge, an attractive village set on a hill. It was the birthplace of the physicist Laplace, whose house and statue can be seen in the square.

St-Céneri-le-Gérei

The Alpes Mancelles is a region which lies about 100km due south of the Auge to the west of Alençon. The French have a fondness for calling even a modest hill a *montagne*, but the term Alpes is really rather over-the-top for terrain which rises to less than 400 metres. It is, nevertheless, a delightful region, forming part of the Parc Régional de Normandie-Maine. It encompasses one of the loveliest stretches of the River Sarthe, with wooded

A view of the River Sarthe from the ancient stone bridge in the village of St-Céneri-le-Gérei.

valleys and hillsides cloaked in broom and heather.

The tiny village of St-Céneri-le-Gérei is built on the banks of the Sarthe where it flows through a peaceful small valley. Little more than a cluster of stone cottages, with a church on the hill, it has the atmosphere of a hideaway, although it is very popular in the summer months. The village has been a favourite subject for several well-known painters, including Corot.

For one of the prettiest views of the village, climb the lane to the small Romanesque church (which contains interesting frescoes) from where you can look down on to the old stone bridge over the Sarthe and the cottages lining its banks. Nearby is the small chapel of St Céneri, containing a large stone, said to be his bed, and a statue of the saint, to which girls due to be married within the year traditionally fix a pin.

The village name derives from the name of a seventh-century Italian monk, Ceneri, who founded an abbey in the valley, destroyed in 903 by the Normans. In the eleventh century the site became a stronghold with a château which was attacked by, among others, William the Conqueror and Henry I of England. During the Hundred Years War the château was destroyed by the English.

There is one hotel-restaurant, the Auberge de la Vallée, and a *crêperie* in the village, but there are numerous hotels and restaurants in the neighbouring resort of St-Léonard-des-Bois, also on the Sarthe. There are a number of *gîtes ruraux* as well as campsites in the area.

Ste Suzanne

To the south of St-Céneri-le-Gérei, on the edge of the Parc Régional de Normandie-Maine and close to the Forêt de la Grande

A proud owner sits outside his ancient Normandy house near the village of Beuvron-en-Auge.

Charnie, is the hilltop village of Ste Suzanne. It is ringed by ramparts dating from the fourteenth and fifteenth centuries, around which there is a footpath affording splendid views over the valley of the Erve and the surrounding countryside.

Inside there is a network of narrow streets, an eleventh-century keep and a château built in 1608 on the site of an earlier fortress which had withstood the attack of William the Conqueror during a three-year siege but was destroyed by the Earl of Salisbury in 1425.

In the Maison de l'Auditoire, once the village courtroom, is a museum of local history. The church was reconstructed in the late nineteenth century but retains parts of the earlier building as well as statues from the fifteenth century. Nearby is a fine old manor house which dates from the thirteenth century, and there are several ancient gabled houses to be seen along Rue Belle Etoile and Rue Dorée.

The village was originally called St-Jean-de-Hautefeuille but was renamed Ste Suzanne in honour of the relics of that saint, brought back from the crusades by the feudal lord in the tenth century. In the seventeenth century Louis XIV encouraged local commerce by giving a charter for six annual fairs. During the Revolution the village was called Mont-Erve.

Asnières-sur-Vègre

The River Sarthe flows south-west through the countryside of the Maine to join the Loire near Angers. Downstream from Le Mans is another particularly attractive stretch of the river as it makes lazy loops through the meadows and woodlands between Le Mans and Sablé-sur-Sarthe. There are also a number of charming riverside villages.

The village of Asnières-sur-Vègre is built on the banks of a tributary of the Sarthe in a lovely setting. A medieval humpback bridge spans the river close to a working water-mill. The river here is shaded by tall trees, green weeds sway in the gentle current, and beyond is a cluster of old village houses with steeply pitched roofs. It makes a charming view.

The village has an eleventh-century church which contains a series of Gothic murals. Nearby is La Cour d'Asnières, a large mansion built in the fifteenth century, in which the canons of Le Mans exercised their seigneurial rights over the village. On the outskirts of the village are two manors dating from the fifteenth and sixteenth centuries, and the Château de Moulin Vieux, which was restored in the eighteenth century.

To the west is the Mayenne, another tributary of the Loire, and the tiny village of Chenillé-Changé, some 15km south of Château-Gontier, is particularly lovely.

Troo

The River Loir runs through Vendôme on its way to join the Sarthe just north of Angers, after which the Sarthe merges with the Maine and the Loire. To the west of Vendôme, past Montoire-sur-Loir, is the curious village of Troo, overlooking the river from a steep domed hill.

Troglodyte dwellings are quite commonplace in this part of France, often tunnelled deep into the soft tufa rock, but Troo has some of the finest examples. Much more than simple caves, these are comfortable homes with hedges, gardens, patios and luxurious interiors. They are built into the steep hillside and can only be reached by a series of winding footpaths and steps. The hill is riddled with tunnels and caves which were used as hide-outs in times of war.

The site was occupied in prehistoric times, but the village was established by the Gauls to guard an important route between Paris and Tours. From the twelfth century onwards it was the scene of constant struggles between the English and the French, being a natural stronghold in the valley, and was partially demolished after a series of wars. The château was taken by Richard the Lionheart and finally razed by Henry IV in 1590. Since those times it has been home to a number of artists and is today a place of deep tranquility.

There is a grand viewpoint over the Loir from the Butte, a burial mound of the Gauls. Remains of the ancient fortifications and gateways can still be seen. The collegiate church of St Martin, dating from the eleventh century, has a statue of St Mammès, which was reputed to cure stomach illnesses and was an object of pilgrimage in the Middle Ages.

At the top of the village is an ancient well, Le Puits qui Parle, nearly 50 metres deep, which has a curiously precise echo. At the foot of the hill is a stalactite cave and a twelfth-century hospice. On the opposite side of the river is the church of St-Jacques-des-Guérets which contains some fine twelfth-century wall paintings.

The village has a small hotel, La Grotte, and two restaurants, Le Cheval Blanc and La Paix. *Chambre d'hôte* accommodation is also available at the Château de la Voûte.

A few kilometres to the south-east, near Montoire-sur-Loir, is the village of Lavardin, with the impressive ruins of a feudal fortress and a twelfth-century bridge spanning the Loir. Unlike that of Troo, this castle successfully repelled Richard the Lionheart and his father Henry II but finally fell to Henry IV.

The garden and entrance of one of the many troglodyte dwellings bored deep into the hillside in the village of Troo.

BARFLEUR · CHAMPEAUX · BÉCHEREL
ST-LÉRY · MONCONTOUR · LOC-ENVEL

The Cotentin, or Cherbourg, peninsula is one of the regions of France least affected by tourism. This is, I imagine, because travellers are more readily lured by the better-known and perhaps more obvious attractions to the west and the Suisse Normandie and the Loire to the south.

Also, like all regions which are adjacent to a channel port, it tends to be overlooked by those feeling the urge to get started on their journey. Whatever the reason, it is a region whose charms are not, for the most part, spoilt by too many visitors, and it has a superb coastline where you can still find a beach to yourself.

Barfleur
Barfleur is a fishing village on the north-eastern tip of the peninsula, about 30km east of Cherbourg. It has a wide harbour, which shelters a fishing fleet, surrounded by stern granite houses with slate roofs. The harbour entrance is overlooked by a seventeenth-century fortified church. A broad straight main street lined by fine four-square houses leads away from the sea.

The port is an ancient one, used first by the Vikings. In the Middle Ages it became the main port of the Cotentin, frequented by the dukes and kings of England. Under the rule of the Normans its population reached nine thousand. In 1348, the year of the battle of Crécy, Barfleur was burned and the port destroyed by Edward III of England.

It is claimed that the ship which carried William the Conqueror on his successful trip to England in 1066 was built in the Barfleur boatyards. On a rock at the end of the jetty a plaque commemorates his departure and the fact that his captain was a local seaman. Richard the Lionheart also sailed from the port in 1194 to his coronation as King of England. Today Barfleur is a quiet and peaceful place with a modest population,

The fortified church and granite houses of Barfleur guard the entrance to its harbour.

supported by its fishing fleet and oyster-beds.

There are three hotels in the village and several restaurants and cafés. At St-Vaast-la-Hougue, a lively pleasure port 10km or so to the south, there are numerous hotels and restaurants. It too is famed for its oyster-beds and has an impressive coastal fort.

A short distance to the north of Barfleur is the village of Gatteville-le-Phare, close to the Barfleur Point lighthouse. At 71 metres it is one of the tallest in France, visible from thirty-five miles away, and helps to guide ships into the port of Le Havre. This small village is set attractively around a wide square and its church retains a beautiful twelfth-century belfry. Further round the headland the coastline becomes more rugged and wild, carved by small inlets which are bordered by grassy headlands. The village of Fermanville, with its small harbour, is especially appealing.

Just inland from Barfleur is some of the prettiest countryside of the Cotentin, the Saire valley. The quiet river meanders through grassy meadows where cattle graze, and small villages and manor houses mark its course. The D120 leads through the valley from near Gonneville, with its château, to the pretty village of Le Vast, where the river idles past a row of old stone cottages. From here the D125 climbs to the panorama of La Pernelle, which gives an impressive view over the Cotentin to the beaches of Calvados.

Champeaux

At the southern end of the Cotentin peninsular, the River Cousenon marks the division between Normandy and Brittany. A change in its course meant that Mont-St-Michel, one of the great sights of France, changed its allegiance from Brittany to Normandy, which was the cause of some rancour.

Inland from Mont-St-Michel, just within Brittany in the valley of the Villaine south of Fougères, is Vitré, a delightful old town

The village green in Champeaux, with its well and spreading tree is surrounded by terraced cottages.

Bécherel

About 30km north-west of Rennes lies the hilltop village of Bécherel. Once it was fortified, but only a few ruins remain of its ramparts and its castle has long since disappeared. It is an attractive village with old houses surrounding a pleasant square with a garden. The centre of a busy country market since the thirteenth century, this was once the site of a huge covered market hall, which was replaced in the mid-nineteenth century by a grand wrought-iron structure. After the Second World War, this too was demolished.

There are fine sweeping views over the surrounding landscape, which was once planted with flax for the production of fine linen. On Easter Monday, as a punishment for idleness, the feudal lord of Bécherel had the right to burn the flax which had not yet been made ready for weaving by the village women. During the first fortnight of July a cultural festival is held in the village.

A short distance to the west of Bécherel is the Château de Caradeuc. Built in the early eighteenth century by the Marquess of Caradeuc, it has an impressive classical façade and extensive formal French gardens, earning it the title of the Versailles of Brittany.

which has preserved its medieval character to a considerable degree. It has a thirteenth-century castle, well-preserved ramparts and cobbled streets with many houses from the seventeenth century.

A few kilometres to the north-west of Vitré is Champeaux, a minute village with pretty terraced houses of grey stone, formerly the canons' residences. They are grouped around what looks very much like an English village green. A picturesque well under a spreading chestnut tree completes an idyllic scene. At one corner of the square is a fourteenth-century collegiate church containing beautiful canopied choir stalls and Renaissance stained glass windows, together with a polychrome Virgin and altar-piece. In a chapel are the imposing tombs of Guy d'Espinay and his wife, the founders of the church. To the south of the village, is the fifteenth-century château of the Espinay family.

St Léry

To the south-west of Bécherel lies the Forêt de Paimpont, a region of shady glades and quiet pools. It was known in medieval times as the forest of Broceliande and is associated with the legends of King Arthur and Merlin. The hamlet of Les Forges, in a charming setting beside a pool, was once the centre of a busy iron-making industry.

At the north-west corner of the forest is the tiny peaceful village of St Léry. Old cottages and a manor house form a pretty cluster around a really lovely fourteenth-

The pretty village church in St-Léry with its neighbouring old stone farmhouse.

century church. The graceful doors are surrounded by fine carvings and sheltered by a beautiful porch. Inside is the tomb of St Léry, with a carved frieze depicting his life. There is also a charming little chapel with a beautiful fifteenth-century stained glass window.

Moncontour

Well to the north-west of St Léry, not far from St Brieuc, is the fortified hilltop village of Moncontour, set on a spur above the junction of two valleys. It was built in the eleventh century, occupying an important strategic position. It still has impressive ramparts and fortified gateways which withstood three sieges, in 1393, 1487 and 1590. Cardinal Richelieu attacked the village and partly destroyed the walls in 1626. Inside are many old houses, some with timbered façades lining the steep narrow streets and alley-ways. It has a great deal of charm and is largely undiscovered by tourists.

Near the picturesque, irregular-shaped square is the sixteenth-century church of St Mathurin, which was altered in the eighteenth century. It retains six fine stained glass windows from its earlier period. The Château des Granges, built on the site of the original feudal castle in the eighteenth century, is situated on a rise at the northern edge of the village. The festival of St Mathurin is held at Whitsun and is one of the main *pardons* of the Côtes-du-Nord.

Loc-Envel

Close to the autoroute to the west of Guingamp, about 60km north-west from Moncontour, is the old town of Belle-Isle-en-Terre, set at the confluence of the Léguer and Guic rivers. It is famed for its *pardon* of Locmaria, held on the third Sunday of July, the main event of which is a Breton wrestling match.

In the lovely wooded valley of the Guic, 4km to the south, lies the minute village of *Loc-Envel*, which is little more than a cluster of mellow stone cottages, with a Gothic church set high above on a hillock. At one side of the belfry porch are small slits through which lepers were obliged to watch the service from a safe distance. Inside is an ornate rood screen in the Flamboyant style and richly carved wood vaulting. St Envel was said to be one of a pair of twins who lived in the times of the Druids.

A tiny house in the equally diminutive village of Loc Enval in Brittany.

GUIMILIAU · LOCRONAN
ROCHEFORT-EN-TERRE · ILE-DE-FÉDRUN

A feature of many Breton villages is the parish close, a group of monuments, statues and small buildings, enclosed by a wall, between the church and its cemetery. Usually, in front of the church, and entered by a triumphal arch, is a small square enclosing a calvary and charnel house. The parish close is, in effect, a miniature village for the dead within the living community.

The buildings and monuments can be extraordinarily ornate, decorated by intricate carvings and sculptures. There was often considerable rivalry between neighbouring communities as each would try to outdo the other in the scale and richness of buildings and decoration. During the sixteenth and seventeenth centuries many villages in France acquired elaborate parish closes.

Guimiliau

One of the finest examples can be found in the very attractive village of Guimiliau, 60km or so to the west of Loc-Envel. The calvary is one of the largest and most unusual in the whole region. It was built between 1581 and 1588 and contains over two hundred intricately carved, and often grotesque, figures depicting scenes from the life of Jesus and Breton legend.

The church dates from the sixteenth century, but was rebuilt in flamboyant Gothic style in the seventeenth, and all that remains of the original building is the bell tower. The porch, containing many statues based on biblical scenes, is particularly beautiful, and the interior is richly furnished and decorated.

The neighbouring villages of Lampaul-Guimiliau and St-Thégonnec also have outstanding closes, the latter possessing an exceptionally large and impressive triumphal arch.

About 40km south-west of Guimiliau, on the tip of a small peninsula at the mouth of

The parish close of Guimiliau in northern Brittany.
(Opposite) The decorative tower of Locronan's fifteenth-century church.

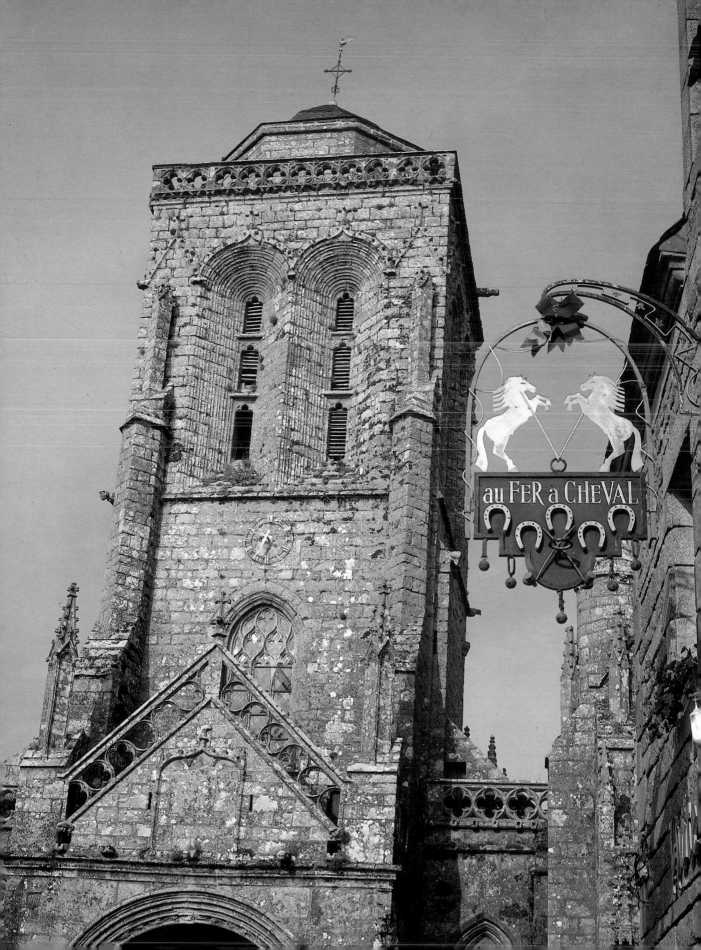

the River Aulne, is the little village of Landévennec. A road winds steeply down through wooded hillsides to the sheltered waterside community with a stunning view of the bay. Nearby are the derelict ruins of a Benedictine abbey.

Locronan

Due south of Landévennec, to the east of Douarnenez, is the village of Locronan, one of the most visited in Brittany. In its centre is a beautiful square, complete with an ancient well and surrounded by elegant granite houses and a fine old church. The small lanes leading off the square contain many sixteenth-century houses. From May onwards the grey granite village is made vivid by the brilliant colour of thousands of geraniums.

The church of St Ronan dates from the fifteenth century and contains many fine

This elegant granite merchant's houses in Locronan is now a boulangèrie.

statues. It was built on the site of a former priiory church which preserved the relics of St Ronan. He was an Irish monk who lived here in the fifth century as a missionary and was responsible for making many converts to Christianity in this remote corner of France. Legend has it that he died in St-Brieuc and his body was miraculously carried westwards on a cart drawn by two wild buffaloes.

A small chapel was built at the beginning of the sixteenth century to house his tomb, which is surmounted by a statue of the saint. It was carved by a master mason of Quimper cathedral in the same Kersanton granite used for many of the Breton calvaries. There is a stained glass window depicting scenes from the saint's life. The village, and St Ronan's relics, were an important place of pilgrimage for many centuries.

The village was a prosperous one during

Detail of a house in Ile-de-Fédrun with the characteristic thatch of La Grande Brière.

Rochefort-en-Terre

About 150km south-east of Locronan, between Les Landes de Landeaux and the valley of the Vilaine east of Vannes, is Rochefort-en-Terre. Like Locronan, it is a quite exquisite little village of turreted granite houses which become a backdrop for a quite spectacular floral display while the geraniums are in bloom. It is set on a rocky outcrop in a very beautiful pocket of the Morbihan countryside, surrounded by deep wooded valleys and small trout rivers.

The feudal castle, owned by the Rochefort family since the twelfth century, saw plenty of action in the Revolution and after several battles was finally destroyed in 1793. At the beginning of this century its remains were incorporated, by an American artist, into the present château, which can be visited. There is a collection of Quimper porcelain virgins, sixteenth-century Flemish tapestries and, in an adjoining pavilion, a small museum of regional artefacts. There are splendid views over the Gueuzon valley from the terrace at the rear of the château.

The church of Notre-dame-de-Tronchaye dates from the twelfth century but was greatly enlarged and altered later. The word *tronchaye* means clump of trees, and the name derives from an ancient statue of the virgin which was discovered in the hollow of a tree during the twelfth century, having been hidden there during the Norman invasion. The statue is displayed on the seventeenth-century altarpiece and is the subject of an annual pilgrimage on the first Sunday after 14 August. Some of the village houses date from the twelfth and fourteenth centuries, and there is a fifteenth-century calvary.

There are no hotels in the village but there are several cafés and restaurants, and a number of *gîtes ruraux* and *chambres d'hôte* are

the Middle Ages, weaving cloth and making sails for the French navy. The trade fell into decline in the eighteenth century, however, with the setting up of a large factory in Brest. Many of the fine merchants' houses are now craft workshops where you can watch weavers at work and buy handwoven fabrics, pottery, glassware and wood sculptures.

To the east of the village is the Montagne de Locronan, rising to nearly 340 metres. From here there are panoramic views of the Bay of Douarnenez, the Cap de la Chèvre, the Crozon peninsula and the peak of Menez Hom. It was here that St Ronan lived in his hermitage, and today it is the location for the Grande Tromenie, a *pardon* which is held every six years. The next will be in 1995, but a smaller procession takes place annually on the second and third Sundays in July, tracing the daily barefoot walk made by St Ronan.

There are two hotels in Locronan and several restaurants and cafés. A kilometre or so to the north-east is the seventeenth-century Manoir de Moellien, a building of considerable charm which is now a comfortable hotel.

*One of the 'ports' of La Grande Brière near
the village of Ile-de-Fédrun.*

all available in the surrounding area.

Gourmets may be interested to know that there is a small hotel-restaurant, Le Bretagne, with two *Michelin* rosettes in the village of Questembert, about 10km to the south-west. Still further south-west, beyond Muzillac, is a hotel in a very attractive and peaceful setting at the Pointe de Pen-Lan at the mouth of the Vilaine. The Domaine de Rochevilaine is a luxury hotel set among a small group of granite buildings originally built to defend the estuary.

Ile-de-Fédrun

About 60km due south of Rochefort-en-Terre, on the north bank of the Loire estuary, is a curious region of salt marshes called La Grande Brière. Once a primeval forest, the region was encroached upon by the sea and the alluvial deposits left by the Loire. In the fifteenth century the land was drained, leaving rich deposits of peat and reed beds and creating local industries and good fishing in the remaining open stretches of water. Even today, although roads criss-cross the marshes, the typical flat-bottomed boats, called *blins*, are still used, and hunting, fishing, thatching and basket making is still carried on.

It is fascinating to take boat trips on the marshes, slipping through narrow lanes of water lined by reeds and irises into vast open lakes which are still and silent. Dotted around the edge of the marshes are a number of small 'ports' with rows of flat-bottomed boats for hire.

One of these ports is at Ile-de-Fédrun, an islet linked to the main road near St Joachim by two bridges. The main street of the village leads in a circle around the island, a fact that is not immediately apparent until you find yourself back at the point where you began. On its way it leads past a succession of

thatched cottages with kitchen gardens and small orchards extending to the water's edge, where they have private moorings.

Some of the houses are very old and almost derelict; others have been lovingly restored. One has been converted into a small museum, its interior decorated and furnished to show the traditional way of life of the Brierons. Another house has a collection of brides' head-dresses using wax flowers, the product of a local industry which was established in St Joachim in the nineteenth century. There are no hotels in Ile-de-Fédrun, but there are many to choose from at the resort of La Baule, about half an hour's drive to the south-west.

On the western edge of the marsh is Kerhinet, another small community of thatched cottages which have been restored. A few kilometres to the south-west is Guérande, a well-preserved walled town overlooking the salt flats, once a source of considerable wealth to the region. Its ramparts are almost intact and the town still has a distinctly medieval appearance.

Geraniums flank the distinctive doorway of this house in Rochefort-en-Terre.

CHAPTER TWO

NORTH-EAST FRANCE

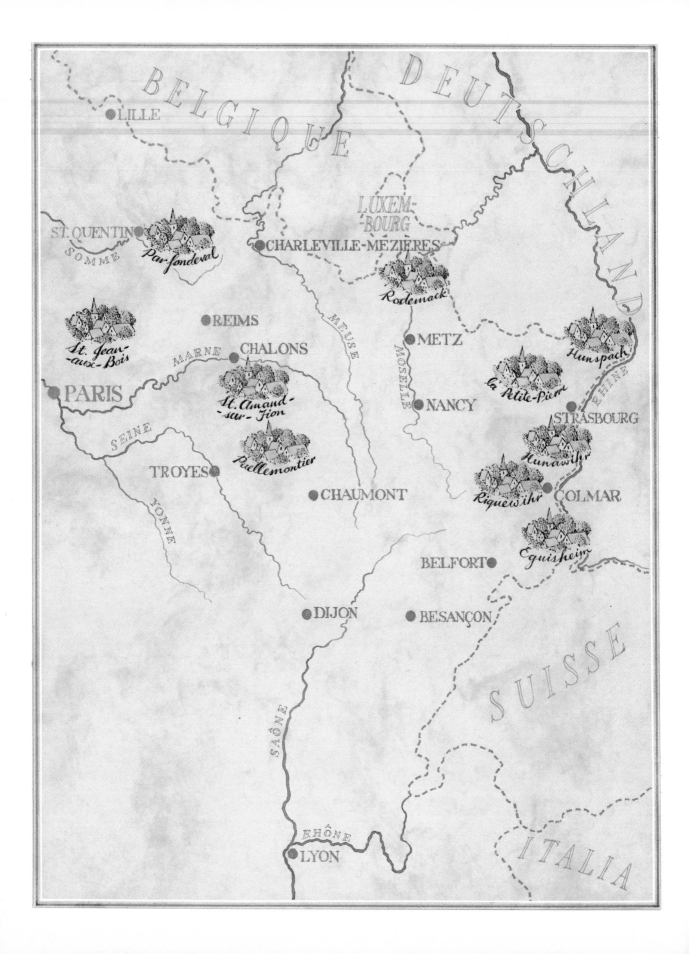

BELGIQUE

DEUTSCHLAND

LILLE

LUXEM-
BOURG

ST.QUENTIN

SOMME

Par fondeval

CHARLEVILLE-MÉZIÈRES

Rodemack

MEUSE

METZ

Hunspach

RHINE

REIMS

MARNE

CHALONS

MOSELLE

la Petite-Pierre

St. Jean-
-aux-Bois

*St. Amand-
-sur-Fion*

NANCY

STRASBOURG

SEINE

PARIS

Puellemontier

Hunawihr

Riquewihr

COLMAR

TROYES

CHAUMONT

Eguisheim

YONNE

BELFORT

DIJON

BESANÇON

SUISSE

SAÔNE

RHÔNE

LYON

ITALIA

PARFONDEVAL · ST-JEAN-AUX-BOIS
ST-AMAND-SUR-FION · PUELLEMONTIER

The Thierache is a charming and little-known rural area to the south-east of Calais, close to the Belgian border and the Champagne region. Here quiet country lanes thread through a landscape of gently contoured hills where black and white Friesian cows graze in meadows bordered by hedgerows. It is a countryside of scattered farms and small villages, with milk, butter and cheese forming the region's main produce. Small groups of old-fashioned milk churns stand by the roadside at regular intervals, and the aroma of fresh milk wafts through the villages. This is the home of that great cheese of the north-east, Maroilles, with an aroma so powerful that a bye-law was once passed in Lille, they say, to prevent it being taken into public carriages.

Until the regin of Louix XIV this northern area of France was part of the comté of Artois, and in many ways it has more in common with the low countries than with France. It was, for many centuries, a border region, and this is reflected in the many fortified churches built along the valley of the Oise. Without castles and ramparts to protect them, the local inhabitants would shelter from attackers inside their church, which often contained bread ovens, chimneys and wells to ensure that they could survive a prolonged siege.

Parfondeval

One of the loveliest of these fortified churches is in the village of Parfondeval, about 45km north-east of Laon on the D977. The village is built on a hill between two small rivers. The sixteenth-century church, encircled by old houses, is entered through a tunnel-like gateway below a small tower and has a tall tapering spire flanked by turrets with slate roofs. The church, like the village

One of the large timbered houses lining the single main street of Puellemontier. (Previous page) Riquewihr at dawn seen from the surrounding vineyard-covered hills.

houses, is built of brick, which is widely used in Flanders. The old bricks were baked in a way which produced a great variety of colour, from pale ochre to a nutty red-brown, and were laid so as to create the effect of patterns and mosaics. Within the church are remains of the old bread oven and well. In the centre of the village is a large green with a pond, surrounded by ancient farms and cottages.

The countryside around Parfondeval is a delight to explore, a maze of narrow lanes winding between hedgerows, dipping and rising from one small valley to another. Many of the other small villages have great charm and interest. Dohis, for example, is a very old community slightly to the north-west in the

*The fortified red-brick church in
the Thierache village of Parfondeval.*

valley of the Brune, with ancient, crumbling farms and timbered cob cottages. It has an unusual fortified church with a seventeenth-century *donjon*-porch and a twelfth-century nave. There is also a manor which was once the court house.

The village of Plomion, further north-west, has a very large and impressive fortified church built of pink brick, with a tall square keep flanked by round towers. The nearby villages of Archon and Dagny also have some lovely old half-timbered cob buildings, and at Burelles there is a fortified church with a huge first-floor room which could hold the entire population of the village in times of war. A little further north, at Wimy, is another fine fortified church, flanked by imposing towers and containing chimneys, a bread oven, a well and a large refuge on the first floor.

About 12km north-east of Wimy, almost abutting the Belgian border, is the very pretty village of Wallers-Trélon. In complete contrast to the red-brick, cob and timber buildings of the Thierache, this village is built entirely of blue-grey stone. A broad main street, lined by houses and farms, leads to a church and manor beside a small green. The village is close to a number of quarries from which this stone is produced. In an eighteenth-century presbytery, La Maison de la Fagne, there is a museum of the region, with exhibits explaining the formation, extraction and uses of the blue stone. In the nearby village of Moustier-en-Fagne, set in a pretty valley, is a sixteenth-century manor built of red brick and blue stone.

St-Jean-aux-Bois

The roads to the south-west of Parfondeval lead towards Paris through a countryside which is largely unknown to the tourist. It lies in a wedge bordered by the route leading south-east from the channel ports to Reims and Alsace and the A1 autoroute to Paris and the south. There is much of interest, however, and the landscape is an appealing mixture of gentle wooded hills, meadows and farmland bordered by hedgerows and dense forests.

The old hilltop town of Laon was the capital of France between the eighth and tenth centuries and still possesses ramparts and gateways which enclose a maze of narrow streets and old houses. It has one of the oldest and most beautiful cathedrals in the country.

About 25km west of Laon is Coucy-le-Château-Auffrique, a medieval village with the remains of a castle, ramparts and gateways, perched on the summit of a hill overlooking the valley of the Ailette. To the south is the valley of the Aisne, which flows west to join the Oise on the edge of the Forêt de Compiègne. This was one of the great forests of France and a hunting ground of nobles and kings. It still has an air of great dignity, with long straight avenues and magnificent beech, hornbeam and oak trees shading silent pools and forest glades.

In the heart of the forest is the village of St-Jean-aux-Bois, known in the nineteenth century as La Solitude. A Benedictine monastery existed here in the twelfth century, but the monks deserted their abbey in 1634. All that remains is a charming church in the midst of a peaceful garden with an ancient gateway leading into the small courtyard of the abbey. Narrow lanes lined by creeper-clad cottages lead away from the church towards the forest, which almost seems to envelop the village.

There is a delightfully atmospheric auberge, La Bonne Idée, which has a fine restaurant. It serves excellent traditional

French food in a comfortable setting with that old-fashioned and unpretentious style which seems increasingly hard to find in the wake of *nouvelle cuisine*. The forest is dotted with a number of enticing auberges, making it an ideal place for a quiet weekend of forest walks and good food.

To the south-east, on the edge of the forest, is the attractive old town of Pierre-fonds, which has a large and imposing château with a mass of turrets and towers rising above the rooftops. It was first built in the twelfth century, but over the centuries it fell into ruins and was finally bought by

A grand farmhouse (top) in the sprawling village of St-Amand-sur-Fion. (Below) This cottage in Wallers-Trélon is built in the distinctive local blue-grey stone.

Napoleon I for a pittance at the beginning of the nineteenth century. In 1857 Napoleon III authorized its restoration under the direction of Viollet-le-duc, and the result is an impressive and fascinating building to visit.

Longpont is a picturesque little village on the eastern edge of the Forêt de Retz, which lies to the south-east of Pierrefonds. At the approach to the village is a striking fortified gateway, equipped with towers with steep conical roofs, and modelled on the cathedral at Soissons. It was built in the fourteenth century to house a small garrison stationed in Longpont to protect the Cistercian abbey

The turreted entrance gate leads into the village of Longpont.

around which the village was built. The village was badly damaged during the First World War and suffered bomb damage in 1940, but has been carefully restored.

The gateway leads into a small cobbled street lined by old stone houses and a large square overlooked by the romantic ruins of the abbey. This was founded in the twelfth century by the Bishop of Soissons but was destroyed in 1830. Close by are eighteenth-century monastic buildings in a fine park containing a lake. It can be visited at weekends and national holidays from 15 March to 15 November. Longpont has a pleasant little hotel, L'Abbaye, belonging to the Logis et Auberges de France network.

At the neighbouring village of Sept-monts, to the north-east, you can see the ruins of a château built by the Bishop of Soissons in the fourteenth century, with a tall keep surmounted by conical towers.

St-Amand-sur-Fion

To the south of the Forêt de Retz is the valley of the Marne, the river of the Champagne region. A pretty road winds eastwards along the north bank of the river from Crouttes, through Château-Thierry, up into the heart of the Champagne region. Although the valley sides are planted with vines along most of its course, the best of the champagne vineyards begin to the east of Château-Thierry around villages such as Dormans, Verneuil and Châtillon-sur-Marne. North of the river between Epernay and Reims is the Montagne de Reims, a relatively modest rise in the terrain which, nevertheless, appears quite lofty in contrast to the table-flat plain of Champagne.

From here there are some fine views of the vineyards and river, and one of the most pleasing is from Hautvillers, a village on the hillside opposite the wine town of Epernay. This was the home of Dom Perignon, cellar-master to the Benedictine abbey around which the village developed. He was largely responsible for the technique of blending the wine from different grape types to improve the balance and quality of the wine.

Two black grape varieties are used, Pinot Noir and Pinot Meunier, these are grown mainly on the Montagne de Reims and on the hillsides along the Marne valley. The white grape, Chardonnay, is grown on the lower ground which extends from the south bank of the Marne, known as the Côtes des Blancs, around villages such as Cramant, Avize, Oger and Vertus. These villages are built at the foot of a ridge of hills south of Epernay, and to the east the plain, tinged gold by wheat-fields, reaches away to infinity.

The village of St-Amand-sur-Fion is situated to the east of the Marne about 10km north of Vitry-le-François. This is a most unusual village, consisting mainly of large half-timbered farmhouses surrounded by gardens and orchards. The houses and outbuildings are constructed around a large central courtyard which is completely enclosed but for a tunnel-like gateway. The village covers a large area, as many of the houses are widely spaced and set back from the lanes which radiate from the single main street. The surrounding countryside is planted with wheat and dotted with huge silos where the grain is stored, but this too was once a wine-growing area.

The village was once the property of the bishops of Châlons. When the Romanesque church they built here was destroyed by fire in 1230, it was replaced by a new church in the Gothic style. The little River Fion which runs through the village was thought to have miraculous powers, so children with stomach illnesses were plunged into it to effect what must have been a rather chilly cure.

There are two hotels and a nice restaurant set in an ancient mill beside the river. A grand agricultural fair and animal market is held in the village on the third Sunday in June, and a *son et lumière* presentation is mounted at the end of August.

To the north-east of St-Amand, between the plain of Champagne and the hills of Lorraine, is an unspoiled wooded region called the Argonne, once an autonomous county administered by the bishops of Châlons, Reims and Verdun. Here, high on a ridge like an island in the Forêt de Beaulieu is the little village of Beaulieu-en-Argonne.

This was the site of an ancient Benedictine abbey, a peaceful retreat hidden deep in the forest. A single street is lined by timber-framed cottages and old stone houses decked with flowers and creepers. In one of the buildings, part of the abbey dependencies, is an ancient *pressoir*, an enormous construction of crude wooden beams dating from the thirteenth century, with which the monks could press 3,000 kilos of grapes at a time, yielding 600 litres of juice. There is a small hotel in the village, with a terrace looking out over the forest, and a number of *gîtes ruraux*.

Puellemontier

To the south-east of St-Amand is a region known as the Der. It was once a vast forest, the name Der stemming from the Celtic word for oak tree. It is now the location of the largest artificial lake in France, which was created in 1974 to help regulate the flow of the Marne and the Seine. The three villages of Chantecoq, Champaubert-aux-Bois and Nuisement were drowned in the process, but some of the most interesting buildings have been reconstructed to create a museum of

local life in the pleasant village of Ste-Marie-du-Lac on the north shore of the lake. There are a couple of cafés and restaurants and an interesting old hotel in the village.

Beyond the southern shore of the lake, a few kilometres to the west of Montier-en-Der, is the tiny, and very picturesque, village of Puellemontier. A single main street, with wide grass verges, is bordered by rows of ancient timbered farmhouses and cottages, and at the end of the village is a pretty church dating from the twelfth century.

The churches of this region are very distinctive, built of timber and cob and surmounted by tall pointed spires. The neighbouring village of Lentilles has one of the most appealing. It dates from the sixteenth century, and has a wooden porch decorated with a statue of St Jacques. This too is a very pretty village, with a broad main street and many ancient timbered houses standing in gardens filled with wild flowers.

The small church of the nearby village of Bailly-le-Franc is particularly charming, and at Chavanges, a rather larger village with shops, cafés and restaurants, an attractive group of old timbered houses surrounds a fifteenth-century church.

An ancient house with its pretty lace curtains in the village of Lentilles.

RODEMACK · LA PETITE-PIERRE · HUNSPACH
HUNAWIHR · RIQUEWIHR · EGUISHEIM

In front of the rugged Vosges mountains with their wooded slopes is a beautiful area of half-timbered houses swathed in red geraniums and row upon row of neatly contoured vineyards stretching up and over the hills. This is the romantic, fairy-tale region of Alsace.

Rodemack

In the valley of the Moselle, just a few kilometres west of the river and south of the Luxembourg border, is the village of Rodemack. The village name derives from Rhoete Marck, meaning the border of the land of the Rhoetes, an ancient Celtic tribe. In the Middle Ages, the village and its castle were the centre of a powerful feudal domain, the lords of Rodemack being landowners of the county of Luxembourg.

The village retains narrow winding streets lined by ancient houses and the castle, largely restored in the seventeenth century, still stands imposingly at its highest point. Beside the fountain and the old wash-house is an ancient stone cross. There is a fine fortified gateway, the Porte de Sierck, flanked by two round towers, beside a small river at the south of the town. It was partly demolished to allow American tanks to pass through during the Second World War, but has since been restored. There is a nice restaurant, Le Petit Carcassonne, and three *gîtes ruraux* in the village, while hotels can be found at nearby Sierck-les-Bains and Mondorf-les-Bains.

Lorraine is famous for its quiche, and ham, cream and eggs feature in many of its dishes. *Tourte lorraine* is another popular, and delicious, regional speciality in which minced pork and veal are marinaded in red wine and cooked in an open pastry flan, like a quiche, with onions and herbs. Lorraine has one of the lesser-known wine regions, the Côtes de Toul, which produces a dry rosé called *gris*.

The fortified gateway leading into the village of Rodemack.

La Petite-Pierre

About 100km south-east of Rodemack in the wooded heights of the northern Vosges is the village of La Petite-Pierre. It is situated on a ridge which juts out over the forest like the prow of a ship, with a castle perched at the tip. It was the site of a Roman fortress, built to defend a pass through the mountains of the Vosges, which form a barrier between the plain of Alsace and the Rhine valley, to the east, and the plain of Lorraine, to the west. In the Middle Ages the village was the capital of a small principality called Lutzelstein.

The first castle was built in the ninth century by the Bishop of Metz, one of Charlemagne's sons. The present fortress dates from the twelfth century but has been altered a number of times, most notably in the sixteenth century by Georges Jean de Veldenz, who was known as Jerri Hans, and his wife Anna, the daughter of the King of Sweden. In the seventeenth century the village became part of France under Louis XIV, when the fortress was strengthened and a garrison established. It continued to be an important border defence, and in 1814 was the site of an heroic battle when it resisted the Prussian army for three months before surrendering.

Today the village is a lively and popular summer resort, with numerous hotels, shops and restaurants. The old part of the village is quite separate, with narrow lanes bordered by ancient houses leading to the castle which overlooks the wooded heights of the Vosges. The surrounding countryside is excellent for walking and enjoying the pleasures of nature. Near the village is an animal park where you can observe the wildlife.

There is a museum showing the history and life of the region in the chapel of St Louis, close to the castle. This was built in the seventeenth century to allow the Catholic members of the garrison to attend mass in

*T*he church of Hunawihr set on a vine-clad hill at the edge of the village.

what was predominantly Protestant country. Nearby, in the ancient gunpowder warehouse, is a museum devoted to the special Christmas biscuits and cakes, called *springerle* and *lebekuche*, for which the region is known.

Hunspach

As you travel eastwards from La Petite-Pierre, the wooded hills of the Vosges give way to the plain of Alsace, through which the Rhine flows north into Germany. The village of Hunspach lies close to the border, about 10km south of Wissembourg, in a peaceful region of open farmland. The villages here are the stuff of fairy tales and nursery rhymes, with steep gabled roofs covered in red tiles, black and white chequered timbering, carved wooden shutters and window-boxes laden with geraniums. There are so many memorable places dotted through the countryside – places like Hoffen and Kutzenhausen – that a route linking the most picturesque villages has been signposted.

Hunspach is the prettiest of all. Here the houses are set well back from the streets, which criss-cross the village and give it a feeling of unusual spaciousness. Many of the village buildings are farms surrounded by kitchen gardens and orchards with large inner courtyards. The few shops are disguised as ordinary houses, which gives the village even more of a picture-book appearance. Although the architecture of Alsace is essentially Germanic, Hunspach seems also to have the curiously unreal and neatly-ordered atmosphere of Switzerland – and not without reason.

The village was named after Huno le Franc, a legendary giant who is said to have lived in a nearby stream. During the Thirty Years War the village was destroyed and the population virtually annihilated. However, it

*T*he château of La Petite-Pierre with its stunning command of the northern Vosges.

was reconstructed at the beginning of the seventeenth century by Swiss immigrants, and many of the local names reflect this origin.

The villagers have traditionally been farmers, but many now cross the border every day to work in Germany. The atmosphere is still very much that of a quiet rural community, however. The wooden balconies around the courtyards are strung with garlands of maize; chickens scratch around the kitchen doorways; and many of the older ladies still wear traditional costume. There are a number of *gîtes ruraux* and three restaurants in the village, but no hotel.

Hunawihr

South from Hunspach lies the Rhineland city of Strasbourg, the capital of Alsace and the seat of the Council of Europe and the European Parliament. Alsace is one of the most distinctive regions of France, its architecture, customs and cuisine quite different from any other.

The German influence is particularly noticeable in Alsatian food, which is rather more hearty and substantial than is usual in France. A good example is *baeckoffe*, a rich stew made with chunks of beef, mutton and pork. *Choucroute garni* is another typically Alsatian dish, a combination of sauerkraut, salt pork, sausage, smoked ham and potato. Sauerkraut is so popular that there is even a signposted *route de choucroute*, and most restaurants have *choucroute* specialities with some occasionally bizarre combinations.

The region is famous for its *foie gras*, many considering that of Strasbourg to be the finest in France. *Pâté en croûte* is also deliciously different in Alsace, as you can see from a glance at the window of any charcuterie, where different combinations of meats are combined in wine-rich jellies inside a golden crusted pie. Many restaurants also feature *tarte flambée*, a flan made with cream, onions and ham.

Kugelhopf is a distinctively shaped, brioche-like cake flavoured with spices, almonds and raisins, although savoury versions are also made. Alsace also produces one of France's great cheeses, Munster, which is often served sprinkled with aromatic cumin seeds and accompanied by a glass of spicy Gewürztraminer. Alsatian wines are equally distinctive. Predominantly white, they are made from the Sylvaner, Riesling, Gewürztraminer, Pinot Gris, Pinot Blanc and Pinot Noir grapes. Edelzwicker is the everyday *vin de table*, served in blue-and-white pottery jugs in the *winstube*, a sort of rustic wine-bar cum beer-cellar where you can taste the local dishes.

Following the *route des vins* of Alsace is one of the best ways of discovering the prettiest and most interesting villages, since many of these are wine villages and the road which links them passes through some of the most appealing countryside along the edge of the Vosges mountains.

The route begins near Marlenheim, about 25km west of Strasbourg, and leads south through a succession of charming villages and towns such as Ottrott, Barr, Mittelbergheim, Andlau, Itterswiller and Dambach-la-Ville.

Hunawihr is a small wine village on a hillside in the shadow of the Vosges near Ribeauvillé, north-west of Colmar. From a distance its most noticeable feature is a castle-like church set on a knoll on the edge of the village amid a sea of vines. It was built in the fifteenth century and is still surrounded by its fortified wall, behind which the villagers could shelter in times of attack.

The village was established in the seventh century, on the site of an ancient fort, by a

Franc lord, Hunon, and his wife Huna. It is quite small, just two narrow streets and a number of lanes lined by timbered houses which date mainly from the sixteenth century. It is undoubtedly one of the prettiest and most unspoiled of the Alsatian villages, and wherever you look there are window-boxes, old wine barrels and ancient stone fountains bursting with the vivid colour of summer flowers. There are several places where the local wine can be tasted and bought, and the village has a small, simple hotel, La Cigogne, two restaurants and *gîtes ruraux*.

Riquewihr

To the south of Hunawihr, just over the hill, is Riquewihr, rightly described as 'the jewel of Alsace' and one of the most perfectly preserved medieval villages in France. It lies in a hollow between vine-covered slopes, with the green-blue mountains of the Vosges rising up behind. If you climb up into the vineyards to the north of the village, there is a wonderful view over the ancient rust-brown rooftops and timbered turrets and towers to the mountains beyond.

The village was first recorded in 1194,

A quiet corner in the popular village of Riquewihr.

and the village walls were built in 1291. In 1320 Riquewihr became the property of the House of Württemberg. It suffered troubled periods throughout the Middle Ages, was occupied and pillaged during the peasants' war, and was ravaged by plague and famine in the middle of the seventeenth century. The village came under French sovereignty in 1680 and was eventually ceded to France at the 1801 Treaty of Paris.

Two fortified gateways guard the village. The Dolder, built in the thirteenth century, now houses a wine museum, and the upper town gate, with its ornate clock tower, dates from the fifteenth century. The walls of the village are intact and still look formidable. Inside, the cobbled streets are lined by many fine merchants' houses richly decorated with timbered façades, carved stonework, sculptured doorways and ornate iron balconies and signs. The château of the dukes of Württemberg, until recently the village school, now houses one of the only two postal museums in France. Nearby is the Tour des Voleurs, which contains a torture chamber.

The village is, understandably, extremely popular and is crowded with tourists for much of the year. Somehow, however, this does not manage to spoil its appeal, although it is preferable to see the village quiet and uncrowded out of season. There are numerous cafés, restaurants, shops and hotels, and several important wine houses, like Hugel and Dopff, where the local wines can be sampled and bought.

A few kilometres to the south-west is the atmospheric old town of Kaysersberg, the birthplace of Albert Schweitzer. The ruins of an ancient castle can be seen on the hill above the town, and there is a fine fortified bridge dating from the fifteenth century, together with many houses of equal antiquity.

Eguisheim

Just outside Colmar to the south-west, surrounded by vineyards at the foot of the Schlossberg, is Eguisheim, one of the oldest villages in Alsace. It occupies a very ancient site, and traces of Cro-Magnon man discovered in the vicinity can be seen in the Colmar museum.

The counts of Eguisheim were among the most powerful lords of their time. Some of their descendents became the crowned kings of several European countries, and one, Bruno d'Eguisheim, became Pope Leo IX. In 1251 the village became a fief of the Bishop of Strasbourg, and it was fortified in 1257.

The stronghold resisted many attacks and sieges during the Middle Ages, but finally succumbed to the Armagnacs in 1444, when it was almost completely destroyed, together with the three castles whose remains can be seen on the hilltop above the village.

It is a delightfully compact village, completely surrounded by a circular street which traces the line of its ramparts. A walk around this cobbled street reveals numerous old houses and ancient courtyards. The château of Eguisheim, which was restored in 1894, dates originally from the eighth century and was the birthplace of Pope Leo IX. Other attractions include a sixteenth-century fountain in the market square, the old town hall, built in 1364, and the former tithe yards, some of which, like the Marbacherhof, the Augustinian monastery of Marbach, date from the thirteenth century.

There are several hotels and restaurants in the village, together with some good shops and many places where the local wines can be tasted and bought. The new wine is celebrated with a fête in the third week of May, and the region as a whole has numerous fairs and festivals throughout the year, honouring

everything from sauerkraut and asparagus to cherries and carp.

A few kilometres to the west, in the Munster valley beside the River Fecht, is the little spa village of Soultzbach-les-Bains. Like Eguisheim, it has a circular street where the ramparts used to be, enclosing a well-preserved medieval village with many old houses and a church containing a beautiful fifteenth-century tabernacle. The village has a hotel and restaurant.

South-west of Soultzbach-les-Bains is a region known as the Sundgau, a flat wooded area of lakes and streams. Many of the villages here are exceptionally pretty, with ancient timbered houses and farms decorated with balconies, from which skeins of maize are hung during the winter to dry. One of the most attractive villages in the region is Oltingue, where a small museum of local folklore has been established in an old house. A feature of this region is the *route de la carpe frite*, which honours yet another local speciality, fried carp.

A section of the circular street that follows the line of Eguisheim's ramparts.

CHAPTER THREE
WESTERN FRANCE

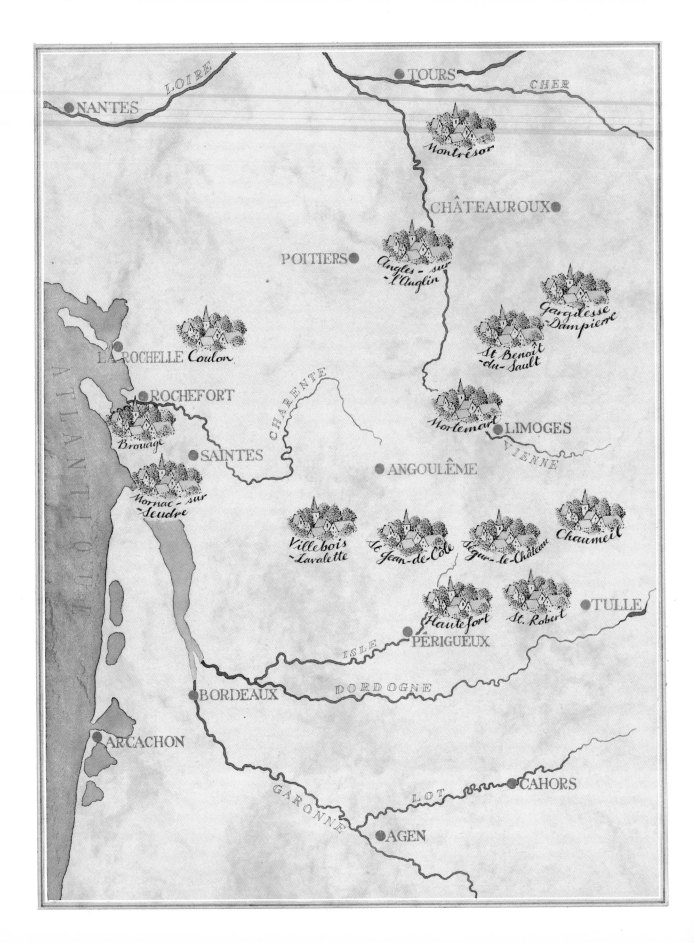

ANGLES-SUR-L'ANGLIN · MONTRÉSOR
GARGILESSE-DAMPIERRE
ST-BENOÎT-DU-SAULT · MORTEMART

South of the Loire valley and west of the River Creuse is the countryside of Poitou-Charentes, a vast limestone plain which stretches from the uplands of the Vendée in the north to the Gironde estuary in the south. To the west are wide sandy beaches which are washed twice daily by the rolling waves of the Atlantic tides. It forms part of the region known as Aquitaine, a watery landscape drained by numerous rivers, including the Sèvre, Charente, Creuse, Indre and Vienne, which thread their way northwards towards the Loire from the heights of the Massif Central.

Angles-sur-l'Anglin

On the north-western edge of this region, close to the valley of the Creuse and some 85km south of Tours, is the village of Angles-sur-l'Anglin.

Some villages are so picturesque that it is hard to believe they acquired this quality entirely by chance. Angles-sur-l'Anglin is the sort of village where one can visualize a medieval art director standing at a distance and instructing the builders exactly where the castle should go, at what point over the river the bridge must be built, and the best place to have the mill.

The village rests on a steep slope on the right bank of the River Anglin, with the church at the top. It spread to the summit of the hill between the sixteenth and eighteenth centuries. On a spur above the river are the remains of a fortress, and below is the old mill. On the opposite bank, old houses are grouped around an abbey founded in the eleventh century.

The village took its name from a Saxon tribe, the Angles, who roamed this region in the fifth century, the same tribe who defeated the ancient Britons. The French have a fondness for giving the residents of even small villages their own special name. In

The village of Angles-sur-l'Anglin with its ruined fortress and old mill seen from the bridge. (Previous page) A detail of the fine timber market hall of Villebois-Lavalette.

neighbouring La Roche-Posay, for instance, they are called Les Rochelais. Here they are known as Les Anglais.

In the ninth century, Charlemagne established a community on the banks of the Anglin. The château, built in the twelfth century, fell into disuse in the eighteenth century and was plundered for stone during the Revolution.

There is a local tradition of embroidery, and the village has given its name to a particular style, called *jour d'Angles*. But, in

contrast, the village is also associated with a rather unpleasant implement of medieval punishment, innocently known as a *fillette* (which means little girl) – an iron cage in which prisoners were kept for years, almost unable to move. It is said to have been invented by Cardinal Balue, who was born in the village and rose to be a powerful and successful figure in the reign of Louis XI. He became Bishop of Evraux and Angers, Secretary of State and a close confidant of the King. He was eventually found guilty of treason,

A view over the rooftops of Montrésor seen from the battlements of its château.

having been accused of selling state secrets to the Duke of Burgundy, and his punishment was . . . to be confined in a *fillette*.

There is a small hotel in Angles, and in the neighbouring village of Yzeures-sur-Creuse, to the north, there is the Hôtel La Promenade, with charming rooms and a good restaurant.

About 25km north-west of Angles is the village of La Guerche, which has an impressive château, built in the late fifteenth century in an attractive setting on the bank of the River Creuse.

Continuing north-west, beyond Ste-Maure-de-Touraine, one reaches the little village of Crissay-sur-Manse, which lies in a peaceful wooded valley. Here there are houses, a château and a keep dating from the fifteenth and sixteenth centuries.

Montrésor

Due east of Crissay, beyond Loches and the valley of the Indre, the old village of Montrésor overlooks the tranquil valley of the Indrois. Set in a natural amphitheatre, the village is built on two levels, with the fortified château at the highest point.

Built by Foulques Nerra in the eleventh century, and altered over the centuries, the château was restored in 1849 by Count Branicki, whose family still own it. At the end of the fifteenth century it came into the possession of Imbert de Basternay, a member of Louis X's Court. The interior contains original furnishings, a fine mahogany staircase and numerous paintings.

From the castle walls there is a fine view of the old village houses below, with kitchen gardens reaching down to the river, which is screened by willows and poplar trees. Some of the oldest houses, dating from the sixteenth century, are to be seen along the lane which

leads to the château, and nearby is a covered market and a building called Le Logis, now the *gendarmie*, from the same period.

The Gothic church, also dating from the sixteenth century, contains some fine stained glass windows and paintings as well as the tomb of the Basternay family. The village has a hotel and a number of shops.

Gargilesse-Dampierre

The region of Berry lies between the Paris basin and the Massif Central and is one of France's traditional agricultural areas. To the west is the *département* of Poitou and the vast sandy beaches of the Atlantic coast; to the east the countryside of the Bourbonnais. The Indre and the Creuse are the two main rivers of Berry, rising in the heights of the Massif Central and flowing north-west to join the Loire.

As it runs from the granite of the Massif towards the plain, the Creuse passes through a valley which narrows to a beautiful ravine between Fresselines and Argenton-sur-Creuse. It is a delightful region of wooded, rocky valleys with small streams and hillsides cloaked with heather. It has an unmistakably romantic character, a quality which has long been recognized by the many artists and writers who have found inspiration in this countryside.

At the northern end of the gorges, beyond the Lac de Chambon, where the river winds picturesquely through a narrow valley, lies the old village of Gargilesse.

The name of the village is believed to come from Gargilus, a Roman senator who formed a settlement here. The village grew up around an ancient château and a twelfth-century church, where some finely carved capitals and, in the crypt, thirteenth-century frescoes can be seen. The houses, many

dating from the fifteenth and sixteenth centuries, are built in terraces on the hillside, and
a steep winding lane threads its way between
them to a small bridge spanning the Creuse.

Gargilesse and its region were made
famous in the last century by the romantic
novelist Georges Sand, who used these lovely
settings in many of her books. She owned a
house here, Villa Algira, which is now a
museum. As the fame of the village spread,
many painters, writers and musicians came to
live here.

The village has a hotel, Les Artistes, and
a restaurant, as well as *gîtes ruraux* and
chambres d'hôte. There is a grand flower and
farm produce market in May and a festival of
harp music in August. On the Sunday before
the 15th of August an exhibition of paintings
is held in the village streets.

The town of La Châtre, to the east, was
also made famous by the novels of George
Sand, and there is a museum dedicated to her
in the tower of the Château de Chavigny.

A few kilometres north of La Châtre is
the tiny village of Nohant, where cottages are
grouped around a small square with an
ancient church and a château which was once
Georges Sand's home. Born Aurore Dupin,
Baronne Dudevant, in 1804, she was brought
up in the village of Nohant by her grand-
mother after her father's death. Throughout
a turbulent and often controversial life, which
included notorious liaisons with Alfred de
Musset and Frédéric Chopin, she returned
frequently to her childhood home in times of
distress. Her writing, blatantly romantic at
first, became more socially conscious, and
feminist, in later life.

The château, where she died, was built in
1760 on the site of an earlier building. It is
now a museum of memorabilia, both of
George Sand and of the famous friends, such

*The stables and courtyard of Georges Sand's château in
the village of Nohant.*

as Balzac, Flaubert, Liszt and Dumas, whom she entertained here. Her bedroom, study and dining-room have been faithfully preserved, together with a delightful puppet museum made by her son. Her grave, and that of her family, can be found in a shaded corner of the small park which surrounds the château. Nohant has a charming little hotel, the Auberge de la Petite Fadette, overlooking the square opposite the château.

St-Benoît-du-Sault

About 20km south-west of Gargilesse is the old village of St-Benoît-du-Sault, perched on a rocky promontory overlooking the River Portefeuille. The village is named after St Benoît, a saint whose relics were kept in a Benedictine priory founded here at the end of the tenth century.

It had been built in a place known as Saltus, a region of wooded countryside which belonged to the feudal lords of Brosse. For two centuries many miracles were attributed to the saint's relics, and the village became an important place of pilgrimage. The prosperity of the village grew after the Hundred Years War, and its religious importance continued until the time of the Revolution, when it was renamed Mont du Sault.

In the Middle Ages, St Benoît had two encircling ramparts, guarded by fortified gateways, to enhance the natural strength of its location. It is a lively and pleasing village, with many houses from the fifteenth to seventeenth centuries lining steep and narrow streets with archways and small courtyards. At the heart of the historic centre of the village, where the remains of the ramparts and a gateway can be seen, is an eleventh-century church. Nearby is the Maison de l'Argentier, with an ancient nailed door and carved lintel dating from the sixteenth century. A footpath running along the terrace of the ancient priory offers fine views over the old rooftops to the valley of the Portefeuille.

There are three small hotels and two restaurants in St Benoît, as well as some good shops. The village hosts a music festival at the end of July and an important livestock fair on 4 August.

About 30km north-west of St Benoît is Château Guillaume, a miniature village set in a peaceful landscape of woods and meadows. It has a church in a tiny square, surrounded by ancient, creeper-clad cottages. Nearby, surrounded by a park, is an impressive château which is somewhat larger than the village itself.

An important fortress in the Middle Ages, the château was altered several times; its present form dates from a restoration in

A house in the oldest quarter of St Benoît-du-Sault.

the nineteenth century. A sign on one of the cottages by the church advises visitors that guided tours are available.

Mortemart

To the south-west of Château-Guillaume, beyond Bellac, is a region known as Les Monts de Blond, a mysterious landscape of rounded hills rising to nearly 670 metres. On the northern edge of the region is the tiny village of Mortemart.

The community evolved around a château built here by Abon Drut, the feudal lord of Mortemart, in 995. He was authorized to do so in recognition of his successful defence of Bellac against Count Guillaume de Poitiers. One of his descendants, Madame de Montespan, was a favoured member of the court of Louis XIV.

In 1330 Cardinal Pierre Gauvin established an Augustinian monastery and college in the village, later to become the parish church. At this time there was also a Carmelite hospital. The church has beautiful sixteenth-century carved pews and a gilded lectern and retable from the seventeenth century. An eighteenth-century covered market hall, with a particularly fine timbered roof, stands in the middle of a small square surrounded by rose-covered granite cottages. A country market is held here on Sunday mornings.

The château was demolished by the order of Cardinal Richelieu, in common with many in France, in a drive to remove the last vestiges of the feudal system. Its ruins, however, can still be seen. There is a pleasant little hotel, Le Relais, beside the market hall.

The old village of Charroux lies on the banks of the River Charente, about 60km north-west of Mortemart, and the same distance south of Poitiers. It is the site of an

important abbey founded in 989 under the patronage of Charlemagne and consecrated in 1096 by Pope Urban II. Possessing important relics, including a piece of the True Cross and the flesh and blood of Christ, the abbey became immensely wealthy from the gifts made by as many as 25,000 pilgrims who came each year in June. It was almost completely destroyed during the Religious Wars, but parts of it were restored between 1946 and 1953. The massive eleventh-century octagonal tower of Charlemagne, which marked the centre of the church, soars above the village. Charroux also has a large covered market hall and houses dating from the sixteenth century.

The timber-frame roof of the ancient covered market hall of Mortemart.

COULON · BROUAGE · MORNAC-SUR-SEUDRE
VILLEBOIS-LAVALETTE

To the west of Niort, in the hinterland of La Rochelle, lies a marshy region of canals, meadows and tree-lined dikes known as the Marais Poitevin. Formerly the Gulf of Poitou, it is the result of extensive land reclamation which was initiated by five powerful abbeys in the region when they built the Canal des Cinq Abbés in 1218. It was several centuries before much more was accomplished, partly owing to the intervention of the Hundred Years War and the Religious Wars. Most of the work was carried out between 1607 and 1658, when Henry IV used Dutch engineers to develop the elaborate drainage systems in the area.

Coulon

The region is bisected by the River Sèvre, creating two quite distinct areas. The Marais Déséché, nearer to the coast, consists of open, somewhat desolate terrain with a dark soil which supports crops of wheat, maize and pulses and provides grazing land for cattle and sheep. The Marais Mouillé, also known as the Venise Verte, is a landscape of meadows and thickets, criss-crossed by canals and dikes lined by tall trees.

This haven of shaded, still water, retaining much of the atmosphere of earlier times, has an undeniable charm. There are few roads, and flat-bottomed boats used to be the only means of transport. Until quite recently it was not uncommon to see a cow being punted along a channel of water on its way to market. Even today the boats are the only means of reaching many of the old stone cottages which are virtually marooned by the waterways.

There are several small ports with access to the canals and from where it is possible to hire boats. The largest of these, and the centre of the Venise Verte, is Coulon, about 10km west of Niort. The village is built along the banks of the Sèvre, and from the bridge

The tiny harbour of Mornac-sur-Seudre is set among muddy creeks and oyster beds on the banks of the river.

which crosses it there are fine views of the old houses lining the quays beside the slow-moving river.

A community has existed here since Roman times, and the village is mentioned in records from the tenth century. There are two hotels and several restaurants, as well as a number of *gîtes ruraux* and camping facilities in the area. There is a museum explaining the life and history of the region, together with an aquarium in Rue d'Eglise.

The little village of Arcais, west of Coulon, is especially pretty, with a small port and old houses on the grassy banks of the canal. The neighbouring village of Damvix is another point at which boats can be hired. Further west, near the coast, is the village of Esnandes, which has a fourteenth-century fortified church.

This is the centre for mussel fishing, and along the muddy foreshore you can see the wooden posts, called *bouchots*, from which the

mussels are collected in flat-bottomed boats. It is a system said to have been introduced from Ireland by a shipwrecked sailor in the thirteenth century. It is from this village that the classic dish, *mouclade* – mussels with a cream sauce – is said to have originated.

The Ile de Ré is reached from La Rochelle by a toll bridge. Near the western tip of this long narrow island, fringed by white beaches with salt-marshes, oyster-beds and vineyards, is the picturesque village of Ars-en-Ré. It has a harbour overlooking the lagoon of Fier, and narrow streets lined with whitewashed cottages.

To the north-west of Coulon, beyond Fontenay-le-Comte, is the old village of Vouvant, held in a tight loop of the River Mère. The site of a fortified château built in the early part of the eleventh century, of which only the keep remains, Vouvant has a church from the same period and houses dating from the sixteenth century.

*R*eturning home after a day's work to a cottage on the
river bank in the Marais Poitevin, near the village of Coulon.

Brouage

To the south of La Rochelle, opposite the Ile d'Oléron, is another region of marshy terrain drained by dikes and small rivers. Here, now land-locked, is the tiny walled village and former port of Brouage. The sea has long since retreated, but Brouage was once an important centre for the export of salt, which was extracted from the surrounding marshes. In the Middle Ages this was a valuable commodity, and the village was responsible for dispatching large convoys of ships laden with salt to many parts of Europe.

The village was built in the middle of the sixteenth century by Jaques de Pons, baron of Mirambeau, and was then called Jacopolis-sur-Brouage. Built in a square, 400 metres each side, the streets criss-cross in a grid, as in a *bastide*. During the Religious Wars the village served as a base for the King's troops against the Huguenot-held town of La Rochelle. It was taken by the Protestants after a siege of several weeks and then re-taken by the royal army seven years later.

During the siege of La Rochelle in 1628, Brouage became the royal army's arsenal and Richelieu engaged the services of an engineer, Pierre d'Argencourt, to renew and extend the fortifications. It took ten years to complete, during which there was a garrison of six thousand men, making Brouage the most powerful strongold on the Atlantic coast.

Brouage is also the location of a sad love story. Louis XIV fell in love with Marie de Mancini, a niece of Cardinal Mazarin, and wanted to marry her. Mazarin, however, wanted the King to marry his cousin, a Spanish princess, and imprisoned Marie in Brouage. On returning from his reluctant marriage, and still pining for Marie, the King and his entourage passed close to Brouage and he slipped away to visit her. Mazarin had anticipated this, however, and had cunningly moved Marie back to Paris, leaving Louis to spend a lonely night in her room.

Today the village has a population of around two hundred, the salt-beds having been abandoned at the end of the nineteenth century, but its ramparts, towers and gateways are largely intact. The forges still stand, now occupied by the tourist bureau, and the powder magazines and food stores can also be visited.

Mornac-sur-Seudre

To the south of Brouage are the oyster-beds of Marennes, created on the estuary of the River Seudre after the demise of the salt industry. The village of Mornac lies on the left bank, a village of low, whitewashed cottages surrounded by a network of muddy creeks and inlets. It is one of those places that has a charm far greater than its location might suggest. The atmosphere of the village has a relaxed and rather secretive quality – more Mediterranean than Atlantic.

The name stems from the Celtic word meaning calm water, and during the Middle Ages the village was a base for shipwreckers. Like Brouage, it was fortified with ramparts and a château-fort, and was an important stronghold during the Religious Wars.

The narrow streets, lined by fishermen's houses, lead down to a quay at the end of a long muddy creek where the fishing boats are moored. A road follows the dike past a row of rickety sheds out to the edge of the Seudre estuary. Here you can watch the fisherman scooping the shellfish from the river bed with nets on long poles.

On the site of a Merovingian sanctuary there is a church dating from the eleventh century and the remains of the ancient château. At the entrance to the village is an ancient market hall with a timber-framed roof supported on stone pillars. A market is held here each Wednesday.

There is no hotel, but the village has several small restaurants where you can taste the freshest shellfish you are ever likely to find. A number of craftsmen and artists are established in some of the village houses.

At Chalons, a few kilometres to the north-east on the D733, is the Hôtel la Galiote on the edge of the marshes. The *patron* is a keen photographer and arranges motorized excursions on to the marshes to see the wildlife. Nearby is the Moulin de Chalons, an attractive mill hotel.

To the south-east of Mornac on the Gironde estuary is the minute village of Talmont. Set on a small promontory in the river mouth, it consists of a single street lined by flower-decked old cottages. At the tip of the headland, on the very edge of a cliff, is the tiny twelfth-century church of Ste Radegonde, from which pilgrims left for Santiago de Compostela.

Villebois-Lavalette

About 20km south-east of Angoulême lies the old village of Villebois-Lavalette, which is built on two levels and set in an attractive region of wooded hills. The château is built on the summit of a tall, dome-shaped hill, and

Looking northwards across the estuary of the Seudre from Mornac where the shellfish are scooped up in long-handled nets.

there are fine views of the surrounding countryside from its walls.

It was the site of a Roman camp guarding the road between Rochebeaucourt and Blanzac, which could be seen for a considerable distance from this lofty vantage-point. This was succeeded by a feudal castle, below which the village developed. The château was reconstructed in the seventeenth century by the Maréchal de Navailles, who had been exiled from his lands by Louis XIV. The chapel dates from the twelfth century and there are remains of the medieval ramparts and towers.

The old village below is particularly charming, with many sixteenth- and seventeenth-century houses grouped around a small central square. An elderly man showed me one house and pointed out where the heraldic crest had been removed during the Revolution. In the centre of the square is a beautiful seventeenth-century covered market, complete with its original stone benches. A market is held here each week on Saturday mornings. Beside the market hall is a fountain with the inscription: ARRIVEE DES EAUX 26 MAI 1850. It must have been quite an event, the coming of the waters. There is a small hotel in the village.

About 25km south-west of Villebois is Aubeterre-sur-Dronne, built on the curving slope of a chalk cliff overlooking the River Dronne. The Eglise Monolithe de St Jean is a cave-like church carved from the chalk. It was built in the twelfth century as a sacred place for relics brought back from the crusades by the feudal lord of the time, Pierre II of Castillon. During the Revolution it was used as a gunpowder factory. The village, which was a staging post on the pilgrim route to Santiago de Compostela, also has a fine Romanesque church, formerly a Benedictine abbey, with some finely carved stonework.

Village houses in Villebois-Lavalette surround a small square and its fine old covered market hall.

ST-JEAN-DE-CÔLE · SÉGUR-LE-CHÂTEAU
CHAUMEIL · ST-ROBERT · HAUTEFORT

The River Dronne is a tributary of the Dordogne and its valley is one of the quieter, undiscovered regions of this very popular corner of France. Upriver from Aubeterre-sur-Dronne the river valley leads north-east beyond the busy small town of Riberac to the pretty hilltop village of Montagrier, which has an interesting Romanesque church from where there are fine views of the valley.

St-Jean-de-Côle

A road follows the quiet river upstream through water-meadows to the village of Bourdeilles, which has a beautiful riverside setting beside a weir. A massive castle looks down to the river over the village rooftops and below it is a Renaissance château. The castle was seized by the English during the Hundred Years War, but they lost it a few years later to du Guesclin. The château was built by the Bourdeilles to house Catherine de Médici on her grand tour of southern France, but she never came here and the work was halted with only three rooms completed.

A few kilometres further upstream is Brantôme, a small town made almost into an island by a tight loop in the river. A large abbey, founded by Charlemagne, is set below a chalk cliff on the right bank of the river, and a dog-leg stone bridge connects it to delightful riverside gardens which are serenaded by the sound of running water.

Just east of Brantôme the Dronne is joined by the little River Côle, on the banks of which is the enchanting village of St-Jean-de-Côle. A humpback stone bridge crosses the idling tree-lined river beside a cluster of ancient cottages. The chapel of an ancient priory, founded in the eleventh century, is set on the left bank, overlooking a small square with a timber-framed market hall and the château of La Marthonie.

The village was destroyed by the English

The old houses and ruined château of Ségur-le-Château. (Opposite) The Château de la Marthonie framed by the market hall in St Jean-de-Côle.

in 1410, and only the church was spared. The château and most of the village houses were built when the village was reconstructed during the sixteenth and seventeenth centuries.

There are two restaurants in the village, but no hotel. (Brantôme, however, has numerous hotels, and there is an attractive riverside hotel in Bourdeilles.) An exhibition of hand-made paper is mounted in the château, and the village holds a flower festival on 1 May.

A few kilometres to the west of St-Jean is the Château de Puyguilhem, set on a wooded hillside overlooking a shallow green valley. To the north-east of St Jean is the grand fourteenth-century château of Jumilhac-le-Grand, an imposing mass of gables and turrets built in the woods high above the valley of the Isle. It is adjacent to an incongruously large square in which huge cattle markets were regularly held.

Ségur-le-Château

To the east of the Dronne, the River Auvézère flows from the wooded heights of Limousin towards the valley of the Dordogne. This is a countryside of quiet surprises, small secluded valleys, rocky gorges, deep dark woods and open hilly farmland. West of Uzerche, the ancient village of Ségur-le-Château sits in a sheltered hollow on a loop in the Auvézère as it passes through meadows shaded by oak and chestnut trees.

Set on a rocky bluff above the village are the ruins of a ninth-century fortress. By the courtyard is a ruined chapel dating from the fourteenth century, and there are fine views of the village rooftops and the river from the path which follows the line of the ramparts.

In spite of the atmosphere of sleepy seclusion which the village has today, it was once an important and powerful feudal stronghold of the counts of Limoges. Jean de l'Aigle, one of the counts of Ségur, was a companion of Joan of Arc and responsible for the victory at Castillon in 1450 which marked the end of the English occupation. The village was also the birthplace of Jean d'Albret, King of Navarre and Henri IV's great grandfather. One of the timbered, turreted houses is known as the house of Henri IV.

During the Middle Ages the community became very prosperous, and the streets are still lined by many old houses and mansions adorned by towers and turrets which date from the fifteenth and sixteenth centuries. There is also a water-mill, where stone-ground flour is still made.

The village has a small hotel and two restaurants and there is an exhibition of Edwardian dolls, wood carvings and porcelain. The village of Coussac-Bonneval, a few kilometres to the north, has a château and a hotel, Les Voyageurs, with a restaurant known for its sound regional cuisine, and good value, recognized by a loyal local clientele.

A short distance south-east of Ségur-le-Château is Arnac-Pompadour, the location of the national stud and of a fine fifteenth-century château. The latter was given by Louis XV to Madame de Pompadour in 1745, along with the title of Marchioness; however, the King's mistress never took up residence. Much of the original building was destroyed in the Revolution, but it has since been carefully restored.

Chaumeil

To the east of Ségur, beyond the ancient town of Uzerche on the banks of the Vézère, is the Plateau de Millevaches. Rising to over 1,000 metres, it is the source of the Creuse,

Vézère, Corrèze and Vienne rivers. Its name derives not from a thousand cows, but from the Celtic word for spring.

The Massif des Monédières is a semi-mountainous region on the south-western edge of the plateau. It was once a vast forest which was destroyed twice by deliberate fires, first during the Roman occupation and later during the Religious Wars. It is now a largely open landscape of heather, gorse and bilber-ry, punctuated by thickets and conifer planta-tions. In the heart of this countryside, set on a wooded hillside in a delightfully peaceful and remote spot, is the tiny village of Chaumeil.

It was a staging post on the pilgrim route to Santiago de Compostela and it has that curiously profound ambience which seems to be a characteristic of such places. In the centre of a cluster of box-like grey stone cottages with slate-tiled roofs is a compact

The simple church of Chaumeil was once a staging post for pilgrims crossing the plateau of Millevaches on their way to Santiago de Compostella.

church built of granite. Inside is a seven-teenth-century altar-piece and a wooden statue of St Jacques. The village has a rather nice old inn, the Auberge des Bruyères, which belongs to the Logis et Auberges network.

To the south of Chaumeil, in a peaceful river valley, is the atmospheric old village of Corrèze, with ramparts, gateways and houses dating from the fifteenth and sixteenth centuries. On the hillside overlooking the village is La Séniorie de Corrèze, an appealing and atmospheric hotel set in a nineteenth-century

college. It has particularly spacious and comfortable rooms and a good restaurant.

On the northern edge of the Massif des Monédières, in a picturesque setting on the banks of the Vézère, is the small town of Treignac, with a Gothic bridge spanning the river.

St Robert

Due south of Ségur-le-Château, beyond Juillac, is the village of St Robert, set among a beautiful landscape of wooded hills to the west of the River Vézère. The village was originally named Murel and later took the

name of St Robert, an illustrious son of the village who founded the abbey of La Chaise Dieu in the eleventh century.

He also founded a monastery in the village and built the huge Romanesque church, to which a defensive turret and a tower were added in the fourteenth century. The church contains a thirteenth-century wooden statue of Christ and four huge wrought-iron chandeliers dating from the twelfth century.

The village commands a wide view of the surrounding landscape from its lofty hilltop position and was a well-defended stronghold in the Middle Ages. It also played an important role during the Religious Wars. At the time of the Revolution its name was changed to Mont-Bel-Air.

There are many fine old houses and ancient cottages along the village streets, some of which have been carefully restored. There is a small hotel-restaurant, the Mont-Bel-Air, and some shops, including a *charcuterie* which sells regional specialities.

A summer music festival is held during July and August and a pilgrimage on 15 August, the patron saint's day. There is a monthly fair on the first Wednesday of each month and a grand annual fair held on 9 December.

To the east are the gorges of the Vézère, and a particularly lovely stretch of the river can be seen by following the road which loops through Voutezac, Alassac, Estivaux and Orgnac. This is grand picnicking country, with chestnut-shaded meadows beside the fast-running river and small cascades tumbling through steep wooded hillsides.

Hautefort

About 12km to the east of St Robert, over-looking the valley of the Auvézère, is the

Old houses in the hilltop village of St. Robert.

fortified hilltop village of Hautefort. The village grew up around a castle built by the La Tours, a noble Limousin family.

In the twelfth century it became the property of Bertrand de Born, a famous troubadour and political satirist of the Middle Ages. He was a close friend and ally of Henri Court-Mantel who, in defiance of his father, Henry II, caused havoc in the region, culminating in the notorious pillaging of the shrine at Rocamadour. In 1186, after the young Henri's death, the King, together with Bertrand's brother Constantine, attacked and destroyed the castle, and Bertrand sought solace and tranquillity in religious retreat.

Marie de Hautefort, another notable occupant of the castle, was a favourite of Louis XIII and a leading light of the court's literary circle during the first half of the seventeenth century.

The present château is a grand classical building, with formal gardens and terraces, surrounded by a massive wall which rises up above the village rooftops. It dates from the seventeenth century but was largely destroyed by a fire in 1968, said to have been caused by a discarded cigarette. Extensive restoration has returned it to its former glory.

The restored château of Hautefort is set high above the village rooftops overlooking a broad green valley.

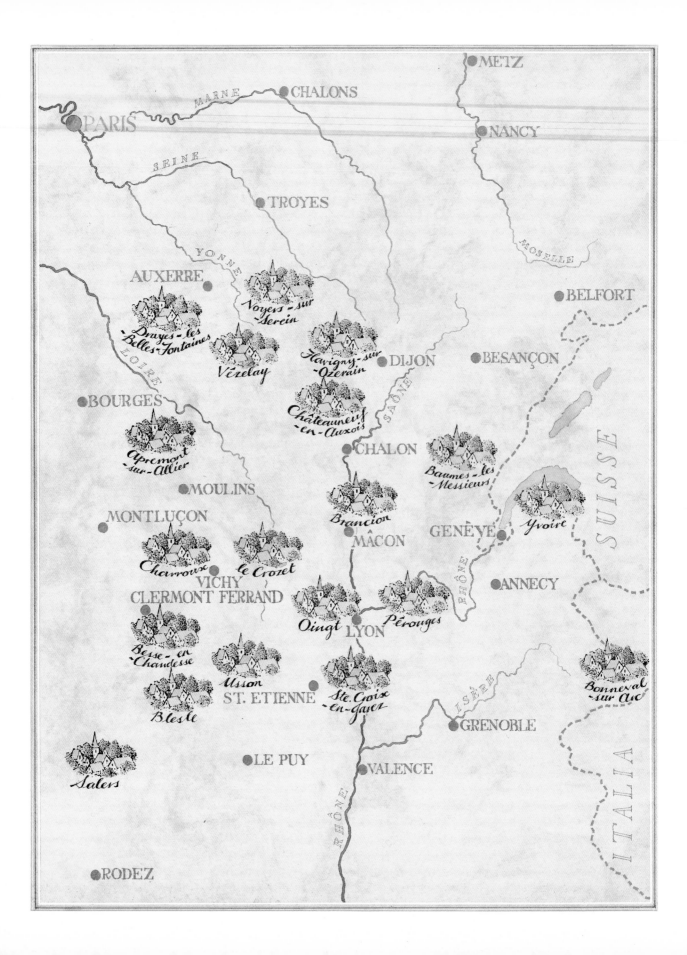

METZ

CHALONS

MARNE

PARIS

SEINE

TROYES

MOSELLE

YONNE

AUXERRE

Noyers-sur-Serein

BELFORT

Druyes-les-Belles-Fontaines

Vézelay

Flavigny-sur-Ozerain

DIJON

BESANÇON

LOIRE

BOURGES

Châteauneuf-en-Auxois

SAÔNE

SUISSE

Apremont-sur-Allier

CHALON

Baumes-les-Messieurs

Yvoire

MOULINS

Brancion

GENÈVE

MONTLUÇON

MÂCON

Charroux

le Crozet

VICHY

CLERMONT FERRAND

Oingt

LYON

Pérouges

RHÔNE

ANNECY

Besse-en-Chandesse

Usson

ST. ETIENNE

Ste. Croix-en-Gaves

ISÈRE

Bonneval-sur Arc

Blesle

GRENOBLE

Salers

LE PUY

VALENCE

RHÔNE

ITALIA

RODEZ

VÉZELAY · DRUYES-LES-BELLES-FONTAINES
APREMONT-SUR-ALLIER · NOYERS-SUR-SEREIN
FLAVIGNY-SUR-OZERAIN · CHÂTEAUNEUF-EN-AUXOIS

To the south of Paris, bordered by the Saône, the Loire and the upper Seine, is Burgundy, traditionally the heartland and crossroads of France. Excavations in Solutré have revealed traces of man's existence here as much as 15,000 years ago. In the Middle Ages Burgundy was an independent kingdom, stretching from the low countries in the north to Switzerland in the east. Today it encompasses the *départements* of Yonne, Côte-d'Or, Nièvre and Saône-et-Loire.

Vézelay

Burgundy is synonymous with fine wines and good food, some of the greatest vineyards in the world lie either side of the A6 autoroute as it speeds from Paris to the south. First, near Auxerre, are the vineyards of the great white wine, Chablis, and to the west, the Sauvignon de St-Bris and the reds and rosés of Irancy.

A little further south, to the west of the motorway, are the Côtes de Nuit and the Côtes de Beaune, producing legendary wines such as Gevrey-Chambertin, Aloxe-Corton, Nuits-St-Georges, Montrachet and Meursault. Next are the vineyards of the Chalonnais, with such famous wine villages as Rully, Givry and Mercurey, and the Maconnais, with Pouilly, Fuissé and St-Véran. Finally, near Villefranche-sur-Saône, are the rounded hills from where the annual tide of Beaujolais flows, as well as the wine from the famous ten *grand cru* villages.

Burgundy has given birth to many classic dishes, the most well-known being boeuf bourguignon and coq au vin, which most people will have cooked at some time or other. There are many equally delicious but less well-known dishes to be sampled. Other specialities which tempt the visitor include *quenelles de brochet*, light sausage-like dumplings of pike served in a crayfish sauce; *oeufs*

The tiny village of Yevre-le-Chatel set on the edge of the Beauce plateau is dominated by the remains of an impressive château. (Previous page) Sunrise lights the hilltop village of Vézeley, an island among the surrounding vineyards.

en meurette, eggs poached in red wine sauce with onions and mushrooms; *gougères*, light golden puffs of choux pastry with a creamy filling of cheese; and *jambon persillé*, chunks of ham set into a wine-rich jelly and marbled with finely chopped parsley. There are some great cheeses here, too, such as Epoisses, Chaource, Cîteaux, St Florentin and Soumaintrain.

Burgundy, like much of France, has a rich historical and cultural heritage, and one of the most inspiring examples is to be found in the village of Vézelay, which lies a few kilometres to the south-west of Avallon. It is built along the ridge of a hill which rises sharply from the valley of the River Cure. At the summit, the basilica of Ste Madeleine is set on a terrace at the northern tip of the hill.

It is the largest convent church in France, founded by a count of Burgundy, Girard de Roussillon, and consecrated by Pope John VIII in 878. The relics of Mary Magdelene were placed in the church in the tenth century, whereupon it became a major place of pilgrimage as well as an important staging post on the route to Santiago de Compostela, and was considerably enlarged. In 1120 there was a tragic fire during the annual pilgrimage and over a thousand pilgrims were trapped in the church and burned to death. The church was almost completely destroyed, and although rebuilding work was commenced soon afterwards, it took nearly a hundred years to complete.

The Second Crusade was preached in the church by St Bernard in the presence of Louis VII in 1146 and it was a meeting-place for Richard the Lionheart and the French King, Philippe Auguste, prior to their departure for the Third Crusade. At the end of the thirteenth century, doubts were cast on the authenticity of the relics and the numbers of pilgrims began to dwindle. The church was seriously damaged during the Religious Wars and again during the Revolution. By the nineteenth century it was in danger of collapse, and a complete restoration was carried out under the direction of Viollet-le-duc in 1840.

The nave, nearly 200 feet long and enormously high, is flooded with light which is reflected from the white and gold stone. The three doorways leading into the nave are decorated by exquisite stone carvings, considered to be among the finest of the western world. There are sweeping views from the tree-shaped terrace over the valley of the Cure and the surrounding hills, which are covered with vineyards. Vézelay has its own appellation of Côtes de Bourgogne wines.

The street which climbs the hill from the square to the basilica has many fine old houses with carved doorways and mullioned windows, and one can still see two of the seven original gateways in the ramparts which encircled the village in medieval times. There are numerous shops, cafés and restaurants, together with several hotels in or near the village. The neighbouring village of St-Père-sous-Vézelay is the location of one of the finest hotel-restaurants in France called L'Espérance.

Near to Avallon a small road leads through the very beautiful valley of the River Cousin, while the Cure, leading north from Vézelay to Voutenay-sur-Cure and Cravant, also provides some delightful riverside spots.

On a steep hill overlooking the River Yonne north-west of Vézelay is the attractive old village of Mailly-le-Château with its thirteenth-century Gothic church. Overlooking the square is Le Castel, a charming hotel with a restaurant noted for its excellent regional cuisine.

To the north of Mailly-le-Château, set in a pleasant countryside of grand rolling hills and vineyards, are the wine villages of Coulanges-la-Vineuse, Irancy and St-Bris-le-Vineux. Here you will find numerous places to taste and buy some of the lesser-known Burgundy wines.

Druyes-les-Belles-Fontaines

To the south-west of Mailly-le-Château, on the far side of the Forêt de Frétoy, is the charmingly named village of Druyes-les-Belles-Fontaines. It is set beside a spring, the source of the River Druyes, which flows into the Yonne. A limpid pool, shaded by trees and surrounded by old houses and a Romanesque church, creates a beautifully peaceful scene.

On a hilltop above the village is an impressive fortress with towers set at the four corners of its ramparts and a castellated gateway.

The castle dates from the twelfth century and was the domain of Pierre de Courtenay, Count of Auxerre and Nevers, who participated in the Third Crusade. It played an important military role during the Middle Ages and had a succession of powerful lords until the Revolution, after which the domain was split into numerous lots and sold piecemeal. At the foot of the castle, overlooking the pool, is a hotel, the Auberge des Sources, one of the Logis et Auberges de France network.

To the north-west of Burgundy in the *département* of Loiret begins a region known

The village and château of Druyes-les-Belles-Fontaines, reflected in its lake.

as the Beauce, a vast plain which reaches away to distant horizons. Borderless fields of wheat and root crops are divided only by roads and narrow tracks, there are few trees or hedges, and the area is populated only by island-like villages and fortified farms.

On the south-eastern edge of the Beauce is the small village of Yèvre-le-Châtel, set on a ridge which marks the limit of the plain and overlooks the attractive little valley of the River Rimarde. This appealing community of creeper-clad stone cottages and narrow lanes is well off the beaten track and relatively undiscovered.

At a bend in the main street is a gateway which leads into a tree-shaded close beside the walls of a well-preserved thirteenth-century castle. Built in the form of a trapezium by Philippe Auguste, it has tall round towers at each corner, from where there are splendid views of the Beauce plain. To the south of the village are the impressive ruins of a huge Gothic church built in the early thirteenth century.

There is no hotel or restaurant in the village, but the nearby busy market town of Pithiviers has several. The town is famed for its almond confection – known as Pithiviers!

Apremont-sur-Allier

Just beyond the borders of Burgundy in the *département* of Cher is the village of Apremont-sur-Allier, set on the banks of a tributary of the Loire. Here the Allier is a broad slow-moving river fringed by reeds, its wide grassy bank shaded by trees. It is a beautiful and peaceful setting, the village houses quite close to the water. On a hill at the southern edge of the village is an imposing château.

The village was an important source of stone, the river providing a means of transporting it to places where it was used for

Autumn in the tiny village square of Apremont-sur-Allier.

some notable religious buildings, including the cathedral of Orléans. It was fortified during the Middle Ages so as to defend the river – it received tolls for safe passage – and was a major Burgundian stronghold during the Hundred Years War.

The village was given to Phillibert de Boutillat as a privilege from his overlord, the Duke of Nevers. The château was reconstructed at the end of the fifteenth century and changed hands several times before the beginning of the eighteenth century, when it passed to Louis de Béthune. In 1894 it was bought by Eugène Schneider. It now houses a museum of horse-drawn carriages and also has a magnificent floral park, with lakes and cascades, which is open to visitors between April and October. One of the gardens is based on the famous white garden designed by Vita Sackville-West at Sissinghurst Castle in Kent.

The village itself is pleasure to the eye. The old creeper-clad cottages and mansions, many with turrets and exterior staircases, are built of a warm glowing stone typical of the Berry region. Small courtyards brim with flowers, and the streets and the little square are shaded by plane trees. The village has a restaurant but no hotel.

Noyers-sur-Serein

To the north-east of Vézelay, in the valley of the little River Serein, is Noyers-sur-Serein, a perfectly preserved medieval village. Within its ramparts are narrow cobbled streets, numerous timber-fronted houses and small courtyards of charm. Throughout the Middle Ages this was an important site on the border between Burgundy and the Kingdom of France, and Noyers was the domain of a succession of powerful feudal lords.

The village's history can be seen clearly in the varied architecture, for there are many buildings dating from between the twelfth and eighteenth centuries. In the Place d'Hôtel de Ville is a fine group of timber-framed houses and arcades built in the fourteenth and fifteenth centuries. Especially picturesque are the triangular Place du Marché au Blé and Rue du Poids du Roi. Many of the houses have mullioned windows, carved gable ends and corner posts.

Although phylloxera destroyed the vineyards in the immediate area, its importance as a wine-growing region can be seen in the numerous cellars with street level access under many of the houses. There is an attractive riverside promenade alongside the ramparts and towers which once completely encircled the village. Noyers is a lively place, with a number of shops, several restaurants and three hotels as well as *gîtes ruraux* and *chambres d'hote*.

The River Serein flows south, from Noyers along its picturesque valley to L'Isle-sur-Serein. A few kilometres further on is the hilltop village of Montréal, the home of

*O*ld houses frame the fortified entrance gate leading
into the village of Noyers-sur-Serein.

Brunehaut, Queen of Burgundy in the sixth century. In the fourteenth century the château was occupied by Edward III.

The church, built in Gothic style in the twelfth century and later restored by Viollet-le-duc, is set on a natural terrace on the south-western edge of the village and can be seen from a considerable distance. From the churchyard are sweeping views over the valley of the Serein, with the distant heights of the Morvan visible to the west. The church contains remarkable carved oak choir stalls and a superb alabaster altar-piece which is said to have been made in England in the fifteenth century.

The village, entered through a fortified gateway with flying buttresses and stone arcades, is very appealing, and there are many fifteenth- and sixteenth-century houses which have been sensitively restored.

About 15km south-east of Montréal is the attractive village of Epoisses, famed for its creamy yellow cheese. It has a fine château, a residence of the Merovingian kings in the eleventh century, surrounded by ramparts and a moat. Within the outer courtyard, together with a round dovecot built in the sixteenth century, is a twelfth-century church. The interior is richly furnished and decorated and can be visited between July and November.

Flavigny-sur-Ozerain

About 12km east of Epoisses is the town of Semur-en-Auxois, perched strikingly on a cliff overlooking the River Armançon. For a fair-sized town with a population of five thousand or so, its old centre is well-preserved and compact, with cobbled streets and small squares surrounded by towers and ramparts – like a medieval village within a larger, more modern community.

Said to have been founded by Hercules when returning from his campaign in Spain, Semur became one of the main Burgundian strongholds in the fourteenth century, rebuilt in the thirteenth century and restored under the direction of Viollet-le-duc in the nineteenth. The north door, known as the Porte des Bleds, has a finely carved tympanum dating from the thirteenth century and there are beautiful stained glass windows.

A fine view of the town can be seen by crossing the Pont Joly, beside the castle keep,

Narrow streets and alleys lead between ancient houses in the village of Flavigny-sur-Ozerain.

on to the west bank of the river. There are good shops, including an excellent char- cuterie with interesting regional specialities, and several hotels and restaurants.

The hilltop village of Flavigny-sur- Ozerain is set in a secluded wooded valley 15km or so to the east of Semur. The village grew up around a Benedictine abbey which was founded in the eighth century to house the relics of a martyr, Ste Reina – the Carolingian crypt contains her remains. She was a young woman who was beheaded for refusing to marry a Roman governor in the camp of Julius Caesar at Alésia, a few minutes' drive to the north-west. Excavations here have revealed that this is the most likely location of the final battle between the Romans and Gauls in 52 BC, the culmination of a siege which lasted for six weeks.

Flavigny is an atmospheric and unspoiled medieval village enclosed by ramparts and entered by two impressive fifteenth-century gateways. Inside is a network of narrow cobbled streets and alleys with many old turreted houses and mansions. The thir- teenth-century church of St Genest contains a number of fine statues, including the Angel of the Annunciation, considered to be one of the finest examples of Burgundian statuary, and a twelfth-century Virgin and Child, as well as choir stalls from the sixteenth century and rood screens from the fifteenth.

The village is famous for its aniseed sweets, a tradition reputed to have begun in the ninth century. The factory which now produces them occupies the abbey dependen- cies, which were rebuilt in the eighteenth century.

About 10km south-east of Flavigny is Salmaise, a hilltop village dominated by a large eleventh-century château. The village is named after the Sarmates, a tribe from central Europe who lived there until the ninth century. The château was built to defend a priory, a dependency of the abbey of St Bénigne at Dijon, and enlarged in the eleventh and twelfth centuries.

In 1334 it became the dependency of the feudal lords of Mont-St-Jean, a domain to the south-west on the edge of the Morvan, and on the death of Charles le Téméraire in 1477 the village and château passed to the rule of the dukes of Burgundy. The church contains medieval tombs, and there are many old houses, as well as an ancient covered *lavoir*.

Châteauneuf-en-Auxois

About 30km south of Salmaise, overlooking the Canal de Bourgogne, is the fortified hilltop village of Châteauneuf-en-Auxois. Everyone who has travelled down the A6 autoroute on their way to the Mediterranean has probably seen the village. It is clearly visible to the east of the motorway with its château crowning the summit of a steep domed hill.

It's a charming little place, very much alive and not at all the deserted community it appears to be from a distance. In the Middle Ages the village was encircled by ramparts and had three fortified gateways, of which the remains can still be seen. The old houses, many of which have been carefully and sensitively restored, date from between the fourteenth and seventeenth centuries.

It is believed that the village was founded by two Knights of St John. The château was constructed by Jean de Chaudenay for his youngest son in the middle of the twelfth century, and the square tower on the north- ern corner of the building is also from that period. It remained in the family of Chaude- nay until the death of his descendant Cathér- ine de Chaudenay in 1455.

Cathérine's brother was Guy de Châteauneuf, the last of the lords, who became abbot of the nearby Cistercian abbey of La Bussière. Cathérine was widowed and forced to marry Jacques d'Aussonville. She was, not surprisingly, unhappy and became the lover of her husband's steward, Giraud de Parmentier. The lovers decided to murder Jacques, and the act was carried out in 1455 with a poisoned cake. Unfortunately for them, suspicions were aroused when a maid-servant also died from eating the poisoned food; their crime was discovered and they were sentenced to death.

After Cathérine's execution the castle was bought by Hugues Grasset, a commoner, but he was dispossessed by the Duke of Burgundy, Philippe le Bon, and the property given to one of his knights, Philippe Pot, who was lord of the famous château of Rochepot,

near Beaune. He died in 1494 and was buried in Citeaux, but the sculpture made for his tomb is now displayed in the Louvre.

The village also has a fine sixteenth-century church with a carved wooden pulpit, and statues older than the church itself. Beyond the village's northern gateway there is a cross from where there are stunning views of the Canal de Bourgogne and the surrounding landscape.

Near the château is a good hotel, the Hostellerie du Château, making the village a convenient and very enjoyable stop-over for those travelling on the A6. It can be reached by taking the Pouilly-en-Auxois exit from the motorway, then heading south-east, away from Pouilly, along the D18, which runs beside the canal towards Créancey and Vandenesse-en-Auxois. The hotel is signposted from this road.

Looking up from the lower village beside the river, to the towers and battlements of Semur-en-Auxois.

BRANCION · OINGT
LE CROZET · CHARROUX

To the west of the wine towns of Chalon and Macon is a region of steep hillsides and peaceful wooded valleys sheltering meadows and vineyards. The hilltop village of Brancion is set on one of the highest summits, overlooking two deep valleys a few kilometres south-west of Tournus.

Brancion

A ruined tenth-century feudal castle guards the north-western side of the village. In the fourteenth century it was extended and strengthened by Phillip the Bold to house the Burgundian dukes, but it was attacked and destroyed during the Religious Wars. From the top of the restored keep are fine views of the Morvan hills and the valley of the Grosne. The castle can be visited on Sundays all year round and daily from Easter to October.

The compact church of St Pierre has a strikingly beautiful simplicity. It was built in the twelfth century on a natural terrace to the east of the village, with sweeping views over the valley. It contains some fine fourteenth-century frescoes and a statue of Jocerand de Brancion, one of the feudal lords and a companion of St Louis, who died in battle during the Seventh Crusade.

The village is entered through a fortified gateway and within its ramparts are a number of medieval creeper-clad houses and a covered market hall from the fourteenth century. Opposite is the Auberge de Vieux Brancion, a pleasant-looking hotel in a fifteenth-century house, and near the village, at the top of the Col de Brancion, is the Hôtel La Montagne de Brancion.

About 10km to the south-west of Brancion is the mellow stone village of Blanot, in a very pretty setting in the valley of the River Goulaine and overlooked by the 580-metre summit of Mont-St-Romain. Inside the village, which is encircled by dry stone walls, are houses adorned with galleries.

The church and manor house in Blanot. (Opposite) A small manor house with its own tower in the tiny village of Le Crozet.

In the centre is a fourteenth-century priory which was a dependency of the nearby abbey of Cluny. Once fortified, the entrance is flanked by polygonal and round towers which date from the fifteenth century. The eleventh-century church is also of unusual design with a tall Romanesque belfry, arcades and a curious spreading roof. Nearby is an ancient wash-house and fountain. Near the village is an impressive network of stalactite caves which reach from Mont-St-Romain to the village of Viviers.

About 12km north-west of Blanot, in the valley of the River Guye, is the tiny village of Besanceuil. A cluster of very old galleried houses and farms built in a pale gold stone are grouped around a fourteenth-century castle and a very pretty Romanesque church with a wooden porch. It is off the beaten track, completely unspoiled and has a great deal of charm.

Oingt

To the south of Brancion are the vineyards of the Maconnais, where some of the great white Burgundies are produced. The heart of this region is the small area to the south of the N79 around the villages of Vergisson, Pouilly, Fuissé and Solutré. There is a signposted *route des vins* which leads to each of the wine villages through delightful countryside of steep hills and plunging valleys. The landscape here is dominated by the dramatic rocky outcrops of Vergisson and Solutré, a region rich in archaeological discoveries from the paleolithic era.

The vineyards here are planted mainly with the Chardonnay, the classic white grape of Burgundy. Then, as you travel further south, the tidy, elegant Chardonnay vines gradually give way to the stumpy, unruly vine of the Gamay, the black grape from which

Beaujolais is made. The two wine regions merge almost imperceptibly, and soon you see signs to the famous ten *grand cru* villages of Beaujolais, which include Chiroubles, Fleurie, Brouilly and Chénas. These villages all lie within a small area, but further south are much larger areas of vineyards where the ordinary Beaujolais and the *nouveau* are produced.

The villages in this region are quite different from the more famous places to the north. Built in a glowing golden stone, they are linked by the well-signed *Route des Pierres Dorées*. Oingt is one of the most charming of these villages, set like a fortress on a hill, about 20km west of Villefranche, overlooking a landscape of rounded ridges striped with vines.

Narrow cobbled streets thread between ancient honey-coloured cottages which, in summer, are decked with flowers. There are a number of small shops and craft workshops as well as restaurants and a wine-tasting cellar. The church, once the chapel of the château, has a fine view of the southern Beaujolais hills from its terrace and from the tower, which can be visited on Sundays and public holidays from May to September.

A few kilometres west of Oingt is Ternand, a tiny hilltop village perched among the vines, with the remains of ramparts and a tower. A short distance to the north is Chamelet, another fortified village, this time set on a steep hillside overlooking the valley of the Azergues. Its single street runs through a series of sixteenth-century covered market halls built on oak columns.

Le Crozet

To the west of the Monts de Beaujolais is the valley of the Loire and the wine-growing region of the Roannais. This region borders the northern extremity of the Massif Central and is a fertile countryside of green hills, forests and small river valleys.

The tiny fortified village of Le Crozet is built on a steep wooded hill just west of La Pacaudière on the N7. The community dates from the tenth century, when it was the property of the viscounts of Macon. In the thirteenth century it became the domain of the counts of Forez, who enlarged and strengthened the fortifications.

The village is entered through an impressive gateway flanked by two round towers. Within are narrow streets and a succession of delightful medieval houses which have been sensitively restored. The fifteenth-century Maison du Connetable, a timber-fronted building with arcades, was formerly the shoe-makers' hall, and is now the town hall. The Maison Dauphin, once the butchers' hall, has fine moulded windows, and the Maison Papon, in Renaissance style, is decorated with enamelled bricks and medallions.

One ancient house has been made into a museum with displays of local artefacts and crafts. It is open from 15 June to 30 October on Sunday afternoons and public holidays. Near the church is the tower of the château, from which there are fine views of the Monts de la Madelaine and the countryside of the Charolais. The village has an auberge, offering regional specialities, and there are several hotels in neighbouring La Pacaudière.

On the other side of the Loire, about 20km north-east of Le Crozet, is the old village of Semur-en-Brionnais, high on a ridge overlooking the Loire valley. It was the birth-place of St Hugues, who was Abbot of Cluny in the eleventh century. In the centre of the village is a small square around which are grouped the keep of the ninth-century

castle, where the abbot was born, along with an eighteenth-century court room, now the town hall, and the very attractive twelfth-century Romanesque church of St Hilaire. All built in a warm ochre stone, they create a pleasantly harmonious group.

A few kilometres south of Le Crozet, on the wooded slopes of the Monts de la Madelaine, lies the village of St-Haon-le-Châtel. It retains sections of its former ramparts and a fortified gateway, together with a number of medieval houses. There is a *cave* where the Côte Roannaise wines can be tasted and bought.

Charroux

About 60km west of the valley of the Loire runs the River Allier, which follows a parallel course northwards before they converge near Nevers. On its banks is the town of Vichy renowned for its mineral waters, and further west, is the secretive little village of Charroux. It is situated on a ridge, with sweeping views over a peaceful rural landscape of fields and farmland. In the Middle Ages it was one of the nineteen manors of the barony of

The little eleventh-century chapel in the golden stone village of Besanceuil.

Bourbon and the remnants of its ramparts, together with fortified gateways, underline the contrast between its former importance and its present relaxed and somnolent atmosphere.

The site has a long history, for traces of Bronze Age settlement have been discovered in the vicinity. The village stands at the junction of two Roman ways, and its name derives from the Latin word for a crossroads.

During the Middle Ages it was a flourishing community with a large population, but it suffered greatly during the Religious Wars, being nearly completely destroyed by fire in 1568 and 1576. After the Revolution it was the county town of its region, with thriving tanneries and wine-making industries, and was populated by successful merchants.

Its cobbled streets are highly picturesque, with their old houses and courtyards, and its

The southern Beaujolais village of Oingt with its ancient stone cottages.

attractions include a covered market hall, a fortified twelfth-century church, ancient wells, remains of the feudal castle and a Renaissance manor house. The village has a pleasant-looking hotel, the du Beffroi, and there is a museum, open every day except Wednesday from 15 June to 15 October.

To the north of Charroux is the wine-growing region of St-Pourçain-sur-Sioule, one of the oldest in France. A few kilometres north-west of the town of St Pourçain, hidden among the vineyards, is the atmospheric little village of Verneuil-en-Bourbonnais. Its small square, with its houses of a pinkish ochre colour and the ancient collegiate church of St Pierre, still has a distinctly medieval atmosphere. A restored tenth-century sanctuary houses art and craft exhibitions in summer, and there is an interesting museum of wine in nearby St Pourçain.

The imposing entrance gate leading into the old village of Charroux.

BESSE-EN-CHANDESSE
USSON · BLESLE · SALERS

To the south-west of Clermont-Ferrand is the Parc Régional des Volcans, a dramatic landscape of conical peaks formed by volcanic action and creating some of the most spectacular scenery of the Auvergne. It is one of the most interesting, varied and distinctive of France's regions, offering pleasures which range from skiing to rambling and the sheer delight of wild unspoiled countryside.

The food of this region is also distinctive, its cheeses and charcuterie being particularly good. Great French cheeses such as St-Nectaire, Cantal, Salers, Fourme d'Ambert and Bleu d'Auvergne make the cheeseboards in this region a constant pleasure. Less familiar are Gaperon, a potent creamy cheese flavoured with garlic, and Cabecou, a distinctive goat's milk cheese.

Two typically hearty dishes of the region which you are likely to encounter are *pounti*, a sort of savoury bread pudding made with chopped ham and green vegetables lightened with eggs and cream, and *truffade*, or *aligot*, a rich combination of freshly-made pressed curd cheese and puréed potato.

Besse-en-Chandesse

In the heart of this region is the Puy de Sancy, the highest peak of the Massif Central, rising to nearly 2,000 metres. To the east of the peak, in the valley of the Couze de Pavin, is the old village of Besse-en-Chandesse. It is entered by a fortified gateway with a barbican and is still partly enclosed by ramparts.

Inside, tall buildings of dark volcanic stone are grouped around a small square from which narrow streets radiate outwards. The ancient Rue de la Boucherie, recently recobbled, contains market stalls from the fifteenth century and some fine old houses. According to local belief the wayward queen, Marguerite de Valois, stayed in one of these, known as La Maison de la Reine Margot. Unusually, this

The distinctive volcanic stone of the Auvergne gives these old houses in Besse-en-Chandesse their curious chequered appearance.

house has a Gothic doorway surmounted by an escutcheon.

The Romanesque church of St André dates from the end of the twelfth century but was restored in the nineteenth. It contains a venerated black Virgin which is taken in procession each year in July to rest in the chapel of Vassivière. There are a number of hotels, cafés and restaurants, as well as a variety of shops, including a good fromagerie where the local cheeses can be bought straight from the farms.

To the east, in a very pretty part of the Couze de Pavin valley, is the riverside village of St-Floret. The village dates from the thirteenth century, when the land was given by the Dauphin of the Auvergne to one of his aides, who took the name of St Floret and built a castle on the site.

The Gothic hall of the old château contains sixteenth-century frescoes depicting the exploits of a knight. In the fourteenth century, the feudal lord of the time, Jean de Bellenaves, built a church on top of the hill overlooking the village. In the chapel are fifteenth-century wall paintings, and the churchyard contains ancient tombs carved into the rock.

A short distance to the north of St Floret you arrive via mountain roads at the old village of St Saturnin, sheltering in the valley of the River Monne. It has a number of fine old houses and manors – doubtless because the village was the former residence of the barons of La Tour-d'Auvergne, ancestors of the Medicis.

On the northern edge of the village there is an imposing fourteenth-century castle which is considered to be an outstanding example of medieval military architecture, with triple walls, machicolations, crenellated towers and ramparts. In a small square in front of the twelfth-century church is a beautiful fountain.

The impressive fourteenth-century château of the Auvergne village, St Saturnin.

rock which rises sharply from the plain and can be seen from many miles away. A footpath leads up to the summit, where there is a chapel with a monumental statue of the Virgin, erected in the nineteenth century, and sweeping views of the valley of the Allier and the Livradois. A procession takes place here on the last Sunday in May.

There are the remains of a feudal castle which was for nineteen years the prison of Marguerite de Valois, or La Reine Margot. She was banished here in 1585 for conduct unbecoming to a queen after an episode with a young knight at the nearby Château d'Orbeil. The sister of Charles IX, she was given in marriage to Henry IV of Navarre, who was, by all accounts, not above criticism himself on the subject of marital infidelity. She led a studious existence in the castle, devoting her life to religious matters, and was well respected in the region, founding many churches and chapels. In 1605 Marguerite left Usson for Paris, and the castle was eventually dismantled by Richelieu in 1633.

Steep winding streets climb the hill towards the church, passing many very old houses built of the black and beige basalt rock typical of the Auvergne villages. These were the homes of *vignerons*, and many have caves entered by ground-level doorways entwined by ancient vines. The church, which is fifteenth-century, is excellent and well worth the climb.

A few kilometres south-east of St Saturnin is the ancient fortified village of La Sauvetat. Partially derelict, it is still almost completely encircled by ramparts and threaded by a warren of narrow lanes. A little further to the south-east, is Montpeyroux, another very attractive fortified village set on a steep hill overlooking the A71 autoroute. It has an atmospheric hotel, the Auberge de Tralume, with an excellent cuisine and a great deal of charm.

Usson

South of Clermont-Ferrand, the eastern side of the valley of the Allier is bordered by the Monts du Livradois. Between the river and the hills stands the village of Usson, built on a

Blesle

About 30km south-west of Usson is the village of Blesle, built in a wooded valley where three rivers join. The village evolved around a wealthy Benedictine abbey founded in the ninth century. Three centuries later the barons of Mercoeur built a fortress here, of which only the tower of the keep remains.

A clock sits above the gateway leading into the small village of Montpeyroux.

Blesle is known as the village which has a church without a belfry and a belfry without a church. This occurred because, during the Revolution, the abbey church had its belfry removed and the church of St Martin was demolished, leaving only the belfry. The abbey church of St Pierre has an impressively stern interior with parts dating back to Carolingian times. Among its treasures are a number of very early statues and religious ornaments.

Numerous ancient houses in the village with carved stone windows and doorways, indicate its former prosperity. There are four small hotel-restaurants and a museum of local traditions and religious art.

About 40km due east of Blesle, on a hillside in the Livradois forest, is La Chaise-Dieu. This village also evolved around an abbey, founded in 1044 by a hermit saint from Brioude. Pope Clement VI, who was once a monk in the abbey, built the present imposing edifice in the fourteenth century. It was strongly fortified with a vast tower and equipped with wells and food stores to enable it to withstand a lengthy siege. This indeed it was obliged to do when it was attacked in the sixteenth century by the Huguenots. The church was pillaged and badly damaged, but the monks – and the treasure – remained unharmed in the safety of the tower. The abbey was demoted after the Revolution, becoming a simple parish church grossly out of proportion with the small community

The hilltop village and abbey church of La Chaise-Dieu.

which had grown around it. It is approached by a grand flight of stone stairs, and inside are fine carved oak choir stalls, a vast mural nearly 100 feet long, Flemish tapestries and the statue and tomb of its builder, Pope Clement VI.

Salers

On the western edge of the Parc Régional des Volcans d'Auvergne, further south in the Monts de Cantal, is the village of Salers. It is set on the very brink of a plateau overlooking the valley of the Maronne to the north of Aurillac. This is a perfect small fortified village enclosed by ramparts and entered by well-preserved fortified gateways.

The houses are built of blackened volcanic rock, giving the village an initially sombre appearance which belies the almost fairy-tale prettiness of the place when seen at close quarters. Many of the houses are in fact miniature castles decorated with towers and turrets. The community was the administrative centre of the Haute Auvergne during the fifteenth and sixteenth centuries, and in the

grand central square, with its ornate stone fountain, are mansions which were erected during this period by prosperous local lawyers and judges.

It is thought that the village name derives from that of a royal family of Naples, and the earliest feudal lord, Astorg, took part in the First Crusade. The fortifications were built in 1428 on the authority of Charles VII, but the château was eventually dismantled, along with so many other such fortifications in the Auvergne, by Louis XIV.

There are many fine Renaissance buildings, some of which can be visited, notably the Maison de Baillage, the Hôtel de Bargues, the Maison de la Ronade and the Maison des Templiers, which contains a museum. The church dates from the fifteenth century but has retained a doorway from its twelfth-century predecessor and contains fine sculptures and tapestries. There are several hotels, restaurants and shops. A small shady park at the edge of the village provides superb views of the surrounding countryside.

An essential excursion from Salers is the drive eastwards along the Col de Neronne to Puy Mary. All along the route there are stunning views of the Maronne valley and the mountains rising beyond. Even more splendid views await those energetic enough to climb the peak. An enjoyable round trip can be made by returning along the Vallée de Mandailles and the Route des Crêtes to Aurillac. The village of Fontanges is also quite charming, hidden in a small valley a few kilometres to the south of Salers. It too has attractive old houses and manors typical of the region, as well as the ruins of a château and a monolithic chapel carved into the volcanic rock. A little further south is the village of Tournemire, where one can visit the château of Anjony.

An old farmhouse in the village of Blesle. (Opposite) One of the many turreted manor houses in the Auvergne village of Salers.

STE-CROIX-EN-JAREZ · PÉROUGES
BAUMES-LES-MESSIEURS
YVOIRE · BONNEVAL-SUR-ARC

One of the most attractive parts of the Rhône valley lies to the south of Vienne, where the foothills of Mont Pilat rise steeply from the west bank of the river. This is good wine country and the vineyards are planted on narrow terraces, held on the precipitous hills by stone walls built in Roman times. It is known as the Côte Rôtie, and at its centre is the village of Condrieu.

Ste-Croix-en-Jarez

In the hills to the west is the ancient diminutive village of Ste-Croix-en-Jarez, built within the battlements of a monastery. It began as a small chapel founded in 1280 by Béatrix de Roussillon, the wife of Guillaume de Roussillon, who died in battle during the last crusade. Overcome with grief, Béatrix took solace in her devotion to God, and legend has it that she was led to this spot by a mystical dream.

A large monastery, built by the monks of St Bruno, grew up around the chapel, but Béatrix continued to live in apartments near the cloister and became known as Béatrix de la Tour. She died in 1307 and her body rests in the small parish church. At the time of the Revolution the monastery was disbanded, and the buildings were sold to peasants in 1794.

The village is in a very peaceful setting at the junction of two small valleys, with the heights of Mont Pilat rising behind. The ramparts which surrounded the monastery now contain terraced cottages, with kitchen gardens occupying the defensive bank upon which the walls were built. The village is entered through an imposing gateway flanked by four round towers and surmounted by the heraldic crest of the Chartreuse. Occupying one of the towers is a highly unusual Logis et Auberges de France hotel, Le Prieuré, with just four simple rooms and a restaurant.

The monastery gardens can be visited,

The minute village of Ste-Croix-en-Jarez.

together with the refectory, the cloister and Béatrix's apartments. The church contains fourteenth-century frescoes and Gothic carved oak choir stalls.

Pérouges

To the north-east of the city of Lyons, a short distance from Meximieux near the A42 autoroute, is the village of Pérouges, situated on a hill above the valley of the River Ain. It is one of the more obviously picturesque of French villages and its quintessentially medieval appearance has made it a popular choice as a location for period films such as *The Three Musketeers*. However, this should not put you off, because the village has considerable charm, its restoration has been particularly restrained, and it has not become excessively commercialized.

A community had been founded here in the fourth century by a colony of Italians from the city of Perugia; hence its name.

During the Middle Ages it was the scene of battles between the kingdoms of Savoie and Dauphine, culminating in a famous seige in 1468. Centuries of prosperity followed, based on the weaving of cloth from hemp grown locally, and the population grew.

However, the industrial revolution heralded a period of recession, by the end of the nineteenth century the population had dwindled to less than a hundred, and the village was in danger of extinction. Like many such villages, it was saved by the efforts of artists who had settled here, and the buildings were gradually restored with the aid of the Beaux Arts.

The village is enclosed by a double line of ramparts entered by two fortified gateways. A large cobbled square in the centre is shaded by a tree of 'Liberté' planted in 1792 and surrounded by fine old houses and a covered market hall. Most of the houses date from after the siege of 1468. Many have huge

An ancient house built from the rough grey stone that characterizes the village of Pérouges.

103

chimneys, exterior stairs and courtyards, and they are built of rough-hewn grey stone. The narrow streets linking them are paved with the same material. On a quiet day out of season you can almost hear the horses' hooves clattering over the cobbles.

The village has a good hotel overlooking the square, the Ostellerie du Vieux Pérouges, several shops and galleries, and a museum of local history and archaeology.

Baumes-les-Messieurs

To the north-east of Pérouges is the Jura, a region with a very distinctive character and landscape. Some of the more unusual and characterful of French wines are produced in the countryside around Arbois and Poligny, two towns on the main N83 road from Lyons to Besançon.

The village of Baumes-les-Messieurs is south of Poligny at the junctiion of three valleys which lead from the foot of the dramatic escarpment of the Cirque de Baume. The village evolved around an abbey founded in the sixth century by an Irish monk, St Colomban. In the tenth century St Besson and a group of monks from Baume left to found the illustrious abbey of Cluny in neighbouring Burgundy.

The character of the establishment changed at the beginning of the sixteenth century, when the simple religious life of the monks gave way to a more worldly and noble existence. It was not until after the Revolution, however, that the name was changed from Baumes-les-Moines to Baumes-les-Messieurs.

Jean de Watteville was a famous seventeenth-century abbot of Baumes who made a reputation for himself more as a swashbuckling philanderer than a religious leader. His exploits included a duel to the death with a

The stone village of Bonneval-sur-Arc lies sheltered at the foot of the Col d'Iseran.

Spanish knight, which resulted in a period in Constantinople, where he became a Muslim. After many years as a soldier he finally returned to the abbey, and died there in 1702 after 84 quite remarkable years.

One can visit the abbey buildings and also a museum of regional crafts which has been created in one of the ancient cellars. The church, which dates from the fifteenth century, contains a beautiful sixteenth-century Flemish altar-piece as well as some interesting statues and tombs. There are two restaurants in the village.

Near the village there are caves which are worth seeing, and at the head of the valley, below the cliff, is a spectacular waterfall. From the D471, which crosses the C de B a few kilometres east of Lons-le-Saunier, there is a superb view down the valley towards Baumes-les-Messieurs.

A short distance to the north-west of Baumes-les-Messieurs is the hilltop village of Château-Chalon, renowned for its *vin jaune*, a deep honey-coloured wine made from late-picked grapes and allowed to develop a flavour like sherry. The famous regional dish, *coq au vin jaune*, is made by cooking pieces of chicken in a sauce of this wine combined with cream and egg yolks and flavoured with *morilles*. The great cheeses of this region are Comte and Morbier, made in huge copper vats with milk from the brown and white cows which graze on the mountainsides.

About 30km north-east of Baumes-les-Messieurs, beyond Champagnole, is the fortified village of Nozeroy, in a picturesque setting on an isolated ridge. It has remains of the ramparts which once encircled it, a fortified gateway with a machicolated tower, a fifteenth-century church and a number of medieval houses along the small main street. To the north of Nozeroy is the valley of the River Loue, and here, about 20km north-east of Nozeroy, the old village of Lods rises in tiers up a steep wooded hillside. Once prosperous because of its vineyards and waterside forges, it is now a quiet retreat beside the peaceful river.

Yvoire

To the south of the Jura is the Savoie, a land of lakes, glaciers and snow-capped peaks. The largest of the lakes, shared with the Swiss, is Lac Léman, or Lake Geneva, of which the southern shore is in France.

At the tip of a promontory near the western end of the lake is the postcard-pretty village of Yvoire. The village was built in the fourteenth century on the site of a fortress and still has a strong medieval ambience. Within its ramparts and gateways, which remain intact, is a warren of narrow lanes, lined by old stone houses, stretching down to the water's edge. On the very tip of the promontory is a stern-looking château; on the sheltered side, a small fishing port, known as Le Petit Lac, overlooked by a church; on the other side, known as Le Grand Lac, a pleasure port and lakeside hotel.

The village has numerous hotels and restaurants which are known for their excellent lake fish, varieties of perch and trout with which the local white, slightly *pétillant* wine, Crépy, goes extremely well. There are also shops, galleries, an aquarium and a museum of local history. It is an unashamedly touristy village but nonetheless appealing, and out of season it can be a delightfully quiet and restful place. In the middle of July, by contrast, there is a regatta and firework display, and a fairground is set up in May.

It is only a short distance south of the lakeside village of Yvoire to some of the most magnificent of the Savoie mountain scenery.

Over to the east, a few kilometres south-east of the old town of Samoëns, is the village of Sixt-Fer-à-Cheval, set in a deep valley surrounded by peaks. The village developed around an abbey founded in the twelfth century, and the church still contains the abbey's treasures. Nothing remains of the abbey, however, except for the church and a later building.

Sixt has been a popular place with tourists since the middle of the nineteenth century. A centre for skiing and walking, it is also close to the spectacular Cirque du Fer à Cheval, a vast amphitheatre of limestone cliffs below the Pic de Tenneverge. After the spring thaw, dozens of waterfalls can be seen flowing from the peaks. The main part of the village is of little interest, but the surrounding hamlets on the higher slopes contain many ancient chalets and their adjoining granaries. There are numerous hotels and restaurants.

Bonneval-sur-Arc

South of Sixt-Fer-à-Cheval, beyond Chamounix, lies Mont Blanc, and flanking it are two of the great Alpine passes: the Grand St Bernard, between Switzerland and Italy, and the Petit St Bernard, between France and Italy. Further south of Mont Blanc is the Col de l'Iseran. Built in 1936, it is an astonishing feat of engineering and, at 2,770 metres, the highest pass on the Route des Grandes Alpes linking the Maurienne and the Tarantaise.

The pass begins to the south-east of the ski resort of Val d'Isère and climbs to its permanently snow-clad summit, with stunning views of peaks and glaciers, before descending into the valley of the Arc.

The first glimpse of Bonneval-sur-Arc, as you approach from the Col de l'Iseran, is an aerial view of a cluster of grey slate rooftops huddled on the floor of a mountain-locked valley. The village is a complete delight. Although in a location for which developers would sell their souls, the old village has been left completely untouched, while a separate tourist village with hotels, restaurants and ski lifts has been built further up the valley out of sight.

Such is the thoroughness with which Bonneval's appearance has been preserved, that television aerials and telephone cables are banned and the narrow village streets are kept for pedestrians and animals only. The houses, built from rough blocks of granite and roofed with slabs of rust-tinged stone, have galleries which are stacked with logs for the long winter months. Cow bells jingle from the meadows, and the village smells of fresh milk and warm straw.

One ancient chalet houses an information centre, and near the seventeenth-century church is a fromagerie. The neighbouring tourist village has several hotels and restaurants. Bonneval is in the heart of the Parc National de la Vanoise and makes an ideal centre for excursions.

*O*ld houses line the street leading to the distinctive church of Yvoire overlooking Lac Léman.

CHAPTER FIVE
SOUTH-WEST FRANCE

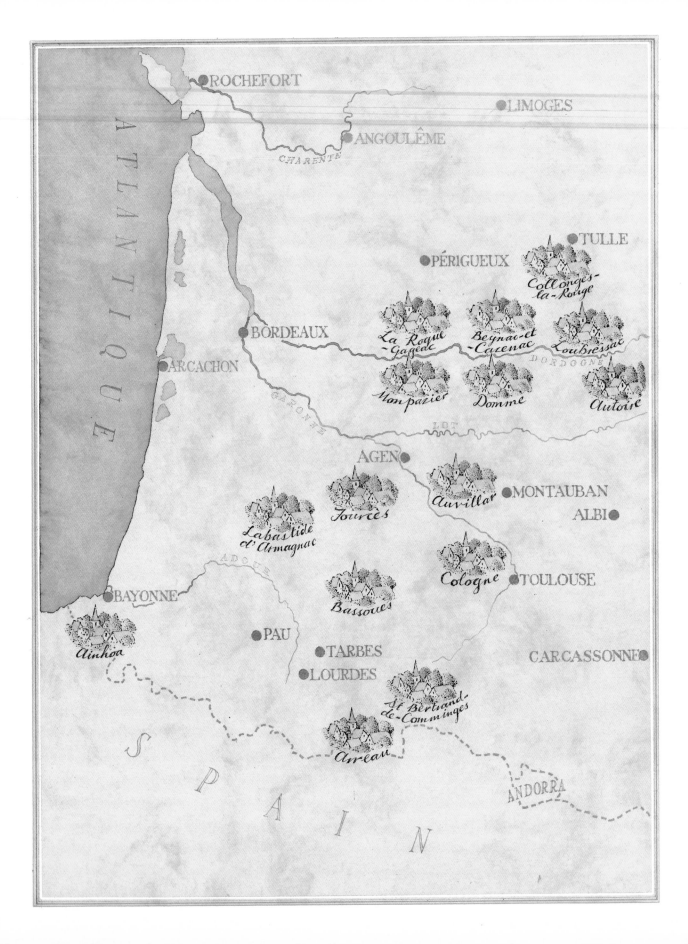

ATLANTIQUE

ROCHEFORT

LIMOGES

ANGOULÊME

CHARENTE

TULLE

PÉRIGUEUX

Collonges-
la-Rouge

La Roque
-Gageac

Beynac-et-
Cazenac

Loubressac

BORDEAUX

ARCACHON

DORDOGNE

GARONNE

Monpazier

Domme

Autoire

LOT

AGEN

Fourcès

Auvillar

MONTAUBAN

ALBI

Labastide
d'Armagnac

ADOUR

Cologne

TOULOUSE

BAYONNE

Bassoues

Ainhoa

PAU

TARBES

LOURDES

CARCASSONNE

St Bertrand-
de-Comminges

SPAIN

Arreau

ANDORRA

COLLONGES-LA-ROUGE · CARENNAC
AUTOIRE · LOUBRESSAC ·

Between the Vézère and Dordogne rivers, to the south of Brive-la-Gaillarde, is a secretive and peaceful landscape of wooded hills and small river valleys. It forms the northern approach to that region most beloved by Francophiles, the Dordogne. Here there is wonderful countryside to explore, with its web of narrow lanes twisting and turning between a succession of small villages where the twentieth century still seems like a wild futuristic nightmare. In summer, shoulder-high grasses line the verges in a lush green countryside of meadows, vineyards and walnut trees.

Collonges-la-Rouge

In the Middle Ages this region, on the borders of Limousin, Périgord and Quercy, was the domain of the viscounts of Turenne, who held feudal rule over more than a thousand villages comprising a rich and powerful little state. This autonomy con-

tinued until the eighteenth century, when the reigning viscount sold his heritage to Louis XV at which point Turenne became an integral part of France.

In the heart of this region is the remarkable little village of Collonges-la-Rouge. It is aptly named, since the sandstone of which the houses are built is a deep rust red. The first glimpse one gets of it, through the trees and across the fields, is almost startling, like seeing a flame in a forest. The miniature city was the residential retreat of the nobles of Turenne, and the extent of their wealth and power is clearly visible in their grand houses, adorned by turrets and towers, giving the appearance of a village composed almost entirely of small castles.

The village developed around a priory founded by the monks of the abbey at Charroux which was destroyed during the Revolution. The church was built during the eleventh and twelfth centuries, and it was

*O*ld houses in the pretty hilltop village of Loubressac. (Previous page) The hilltop village of Curemonte on the edge of the Limousin plateau.

then fortified during the Religious Wars in the sixteenth. The village was a staging post for pilgrims making the journey to Santiago de Compostela.

Among the many beautiful and elegant houses to be seen is the Castel de Vassignac, a mass of turrets, gables and towers, owned by Gédéon de Vassignac, the feudal lord of Collonges and a governor-general of the viscounty.

Collonges is a very popular village and best visited out of season, or else early in the morning or late in the day when the tour buses and crowds have departed. At these times, walking through the narrow paved streets where wisteria and vines weave patterns on the ancient red stones, it is still possible to sense the bygone atmosphere.

The village has two hotels, Le Prieuré and the Relais St-Jacques de Compostelle, and a restaurant. There are also several *chambres d'hôte* and *gîtes ruraux* in the area. A market is held each Sunday morning during July and August, and exhibitions are mounted during the summer.

A few kilometres across the hills to the west of Collonges is Turenne, set on a steep domed hill with the ruins of its fortress jutting from the crest. Narrow streets lined by fifteenth- and sixteenth-century houses lead up to the castle, from which there are splendid views across the countryside to the Monts du Cantal in the east.

About 12km south-east of Collonges is the old village of Curemonte, ranged along the edge of an escarpment overlooking the valley of the Soudoire. The village dates from the eleventh century, and was named after Raymond de Curemonte, one of the knights who undertook the First Crusade in 1096. The community came under the sovereignty of the viscount of Turenne and, according to

A distant view of Collognes-la-Rouge.

Carennac

A short distance to the south of Curemonte is the Dordogne itself, a broad swathe of clear water running between tree-shaded banks which, in the summer, are the haunt of bathers and canoists. One of the most delightful spots on the white-pebble banks of the Dordogne is the village of Carrenac with its steeply pitched brown-tiled roofs and warm stone walls reaching down to the water's edge beside the Ile Barrade.

The village was built in the tenth century around a small church dedicated to St Sernin and was a dependency of the abbey of Beaulieu. A hundred years later it became affiliated to the abbey of Cluny, and a priory and church dedicated to St Pierre were built on the spot.

In the seventeenth century the priory was owned by the family of Salignac de la Mothe Fénélon, and François, the future Archbishop of Cambrai, became the prior upon the death of his uncle. It is said that Fénélon's novel, *Télémaque*, based on the life of Ulysses' son, was written in the village, and the tower in which it is claimed that he worked is still known as Télémaque's tower.

The priory was badly damaged during the Revolution and was sold in 1791. A fortified gateway, the castle and a hexagonal priory tower can still be seen, in addition to the church of St Pierre. This has a very fine doorway with stone carvings and a well-restored, two-storey cloister.

There are three hotels in the village as well as a bar and a café. Down river, on the right bank, is the attractive old village of Gluges with a good hotel, Les Falaises, one of the Logis et Auberges de France network. Near Bel Castel, on the banks of a tributary, is a particularly charming hotel, the Pont de l'Ouysse, with stylish and comfortable rooms

legend, a dozen village maidens were sent to him each year on an ox-drawn cart as a sign of allegiance.

The small community is dominated by the castles of St Hilaire and de Plas, set at one end of the ridge. There are many old houses in the village decorated by turrets and towers as well as the elegant Château de La Johannie and three churches. Near the little market hall are the old village stocks. There are few signs of restoration, and the community seems to have remained much as it was in earlier centuries, quiet and unspoiled and surrounded by lovely countryside. It was the home for some years of the writer, Colette.

Numerous turreted manor houses decorate the streets of the red-stone village of Collonges-la-Rouge.

and an excellent restaurant. For a taste of the château lifestyle you can do little better than the Château de la Treyne, set on a rocky bluff overlooking the Dordogne a little further downstream.

A few kilometres north-west of Gluges is the village of Martel. It has a fine market square with a timbered hall in the centre surrounded by old houses. Nearby is the Hôtel de Raymondie, commenced in the thirteenth century by the Viscount of Turenne but not completed until the following century. Once the courts of law, it is now the town hall.

The Maison Fabri dates from the twelfth century and was the house of Henri Court-Mantel, Richard the Lionheart's brother, who terrorized the region. He died in the house after having been taken ill by a fever, the result, it is claimed, of divine retribution for having pillaged the shrine of Rocamadour. The fortified Gothic church of St Maur, flanked by watchtowers, buttresses and battlements, has a finely carved Romanesque door.

Autoire

Above Carennac the Dordogne is joined by the little River Bave, its valley crowded by steep rounded hills covered with meadows

Old houses and towers in the pretty village of Carennac set beside the Dordogne.

and copses. This valley forms the north-eastern border of the Causse de Gramat in the ancient province of Quercy. A small river flows from the Causse, dropping dramatically for over 30 metres in a series of waterfalls to the floor of a deep rift rimmed by cliffs.

Set between the cliffs on a wooded hillside is one of the prettiest villages in the region, Autoire. Its houses, manors and small châteaux bristle with turrets, gables, towers and dovecots. Built with the creamy stone of the Causse, the half-timbered houses have steeply tilted roofs covered by earth-brown tiles and small balconies reached by flights of stone steps.

One theory is that the village name derives from Hautes Tours, meaning high towers – of which it has many. Another suggests that it stems from Haut Torrent, the cascade at the head of the valley. It is a sheltered spot, and the village gained its wealth from the vines which used to be cultivated there, but Phylloxera destroyed the vineyards in the nineteenth century, and now the valley is filled with orchards.

The community suffered during the Hundred Years War, and a castle was built by the English on a rock at the edge of the village. Its remains are still known today as the Château des Anglais. The story goes that before it fell the treasures of war were hidden there and have never been discovered. The village church, dedicated to St Pierre, dates from the tenth century.

There are two restaurants in the village, but no hotel. During the second fortnight in July there is a grand market of Reine Claude plums from the orchards which line the valley floor.

Loubressac

A kilometre or so north of Autoire as the crow flies, on a hilltop overlooking the valley of the Bave, is the fortified village of Loubressac. It can be seen from a long way off, its ramparts, towers and spires running like a cock's comb along the ridge of the hill. The site was occupied from early times: Celts, Gallo Romans, Visigoths, Moors and Vikings all left their mark here, but the village itself is first recorded in the ninth century. The village name is derived from Luperciacum, meaning the domain of Lupercius.

In the thirteenth century the village was a dependency of the Baron of Castlenau; in the fourteenth century it came under the sovereignty of the King of France and then seceded to the viscounts of Turenne until the early eighteenth century. Ruined during the Hundred Years War, the village was repopulated in the fifteenth century by settlers from the Auvergne and the Limousin, but fell into decline again in the nineteenth century. On 14 July 1944, Loubressac was the location of an important parachute drop.

Today there is no hint of its turbulent past as you pass through the fortified gateway into its narrow streets and stroll beside the mellow stone walls of the old houses which are screened by creepers, vines and country flowers. The privately owned château dates from the fifteenth century but was remodelled in the seventeenth. The thirteenth-century church of St Jean Baptiste contains a seventeenth-century altar-piece and a marble font.

There are splendid views from the village, eastwards towards St-Céré and the valley of the Bave and north to the Château de Castelnau and the Dordogne. The village has a hotel and two restaurants and there are a number of *gîtes ruraux* in the vicinity.

A few kilometres further up the valley of the Bave is the village of St-Médard-de-

Presque. Set picturesquely on a hillside and surrounded by orchards and walnut trees, it has a tranquil life that seems little concerned with the hustle of modern times.

The Château de Montal is 8km to the south-east of Loubressac, a fine Renaissance castle set on a peaceful hillside with a beautiful courtyard of carved Carennac marble. The interior is sumptuously furnished, and there is a magnificent staircase.

About 25km south of Montal is another fine castle, in the village of Lacapelle-Marival. It was built in the thirteenth century by the feudal lords of Cardaillac. The latter is a tiny fortified village, overlooking the valley of the Drauzou, about 10km south-east, where the remains of ramparts and a twelfth-century castle can be seen.

To the west of Loubressac on the Causse de Gramat is the village of Rocamadour. It has a spectacular setting, on the side of the canyon of the River Alzou. The village houses cling to a sheer cliff face, and at the summit are the remains of a fortress.

The identity of St Amadour is something of a mystery, and several claims have been made. The most widely accepted is that he was Zaccheus, the husband of St Veronica, who wiped the blood from Christ's face on his way to the cross. When Veronica died, Zaccheus became a hermit, living beneath the rock where his remains were found some thousand years later, to become the source of many miracles. The village name stems from *roc amator* – 'he who likes the rock'. The village became an important place of pilgrimage in the Middle Ages, rivalling even Jerusalem.

Sadly, the village is now a tourist trap. The narrow main street is littered with souvenir shops, and the terraces above it, which once housed the canons, are now mainly shops and hotels. The ecclesiastical complex is reached by over two hundred steep steps, or a lift.

The hilltop village of Turenne overlooks an unspoiled landscape of woods and meadows.

DOMME · LA ROQUE-GAGEAC · BEYNAC-ET-CAZENAC MONPAZIER

The Dordogne is a *département* of France, of which the city of Périgueux is the capital. To most lovers of France, however, the Dordogne means the river, one of the longest in the country and, arguably, one of the most beautiful. The section of the river which attracts the most attention, and which is usually implied by the generic term 'Dordogne', is the winding reach between the great castle of Castelnau and the giant loop created by the Cingle de Trémolat.

Domme

Perhaps more than any other French river, the Dordogne is a river of castles. Once an important waterway, the broad river is guarded at almost every turn by a hilltop fort. The greatest concentration of castles lies between St-Cyprien and Souillac, and almost exactly in the centre, high above the river, is the hilltop village of Domme.

Domme is a *bastide* built in the latter part of the thirteenth century on the instructions of Philip the Bold. The village is set on the edge of a rocky bluff high above the left bank of the river and encircled by ramparts, towers and fortified gateways. In 1322 the village was taken by the English army of Edward III, who held it for over twenty years. During the Religious Wars, Domme was one of the last remaining strongholds of the Catholics, who were being overrun in Périgord by the Huguenots.

In 1588 a Protestant captain, Geffroi de Vivans, set out to take the fortress. At night, with a group of thirty men, he scaled the sheer cliff which, thought to be impregnable, had been left unguarded. The commando force crept quietly through the streets and suddenly broke the silence with blaring trumpets and rattling drums. In the ensuing confusion the resident soldiers opened the fortress gates and the waiting army forced

A steep street in Domme leading to the main square.
(Opposite) The River Dordogne at sunrise seen from the brink of the cliff.

their way in. De Vivans burned down the church and priory, set up a garrison and converted the villagers to the Huguenot faith. Later, perversely, he joined the Catholics and sold them the village after dismantling its towers.

It is an extremely popular village, and in the summer it is crowded, but its charm and unique location make it still one of the loveliest villages in Périgord. Large sections of the ramparts can still be seen, along with the remains of towers and gateways. Steep streets lined by honey-coloured houses draped with wisteria and brilliant with geraniums lead up to a small market square. It is surrounded by fine old houses and overlooked by the church and the Maison du Gouverneur. In the centre is a timbered hall from which there is access to stalactite caverns which extend for half a kilometre to the cliff edge. They were used as refuge during the Hundred Years War and the Religious Wars. There is a colourful country market in the square every Thursday morning.

Domme is a rewarding place to walk around. Many of the houses are decorated with wrought-iron balconies and have gardens and terraces with tubs and windowboxes brimming with blooms. There is a walk around the ramparts which still give an impression of what a daunting stronghold this must have been to attackers.

For me, however, perhaps the greatest attraction of Domme is the magnificent view of the Dordogne from the esplanade adjoining the butt along the edge of the cliff. Seen at sunrise on an autumn morning, with the valley still shrouded in mist, it creates an indelible memory.

There are three hotels in the village and several restaurants. The Hôtel de l'Esplanade is one of my favourites. It has an excellent restaurant and rooms which overlook the Dordogne.

The main street of Domme is lined with numerous shops in which you can buy the specialities of the region. The cuisine of Périgord is renowned, and you only have to look at the wonderful variety and freshness of the food on display in the local markets to understand why. Walnuts, truffles, ducks and geese are among the main produce for which the region is known.

Walnut oil is used as a subtle and aromatic dressing for salads, and walnut bread is excellent either as a partner for the cheeseboard or spread with honey for breakfast. Truffles are used to flavour omelettes and pâtés as well as being a major ingredient in *sauce périgueux*. Truffles are sometimes cooked whole with *foie gras* in a pastry or brioche case – an expensive treat.

Foie gras is produced from the numerous farms in the region which raise ducks and geese. You will see huge flocks of them pecking in the grass below the walnut trees. The legs of ducks and geese are used to make *confits*, cooked and preserved in their own fat, to be quickly roasted or grilled to a crisp golden exterior before serving. Duck breasts are filleted and served as *magrets*, lightly sautéed to a tender pink, like a fillet steak, and served in a sauce or in its own juices.

La Roque-Gageac

Close to Domme, on the opposite bank of the river, and set below an overhanging cliff, is the medieval village of La Roque-Gageac. Once a river port, it is one of those places where you sense that the builders were simply being obstinate in attempting to create a village there at all.

There is only a very narrow strip of land

between the cliff and river, occupied now by the road, and the village houses are built in a series of narrow terraces, stacked one above the other, tight under the rock, and connected by steep alley-ways and flights of steps. Some indeed are troglodyte dwellings, with the rooms carved out of the cliff behind the façade of a house. It looks a precarious site, and indeed the village was actually damaged by a big rockfall in 1957.

At one end of the village is the medieval-style castle of La Malatrie, actually constructed in the nineteenth century. At the other end is the sixteenth-century Manoir de Tarde, an elegant turreted building. On a rock above the village is a fortified church. There are several hotels and restaurants overlooking the river, as well as a number of

The River Dordogne sweeps past the old village of La Roque-Gageac built against a massive cliff.

shops. In August there is a festival which includes a grand firework display.

Beynac-et-Cazenac

A few kilometres downstream from La Roque-Gageac is the fortified village of Beynac-et-Cazenac, beside a sharp bend in the river. As at La Roque-Gageac, a soaring ochre cliff rises steeply behind the village, and perched on the summit is a church and a large fortress.

Beynac was one of the four powerful baronies of Périgord in the Middle Ages, along with Biron, Bourdeilles and Mareuil. A notorious robber baron called Mercadier seized the castle and used it as a base from which he terrorized and pillaged the surrounding countryside, posing as a supporter of the English king, Richard the Lionheart. During the Albigensian crusade in 1214, Simon de Montfort captured the castle and dismantled it, as he had done with many others.

Within the century a baron of Beynac had rebuilt the castle, in much the form that it appears today. During the Hundred Years War, Beynac, along with the rest of Aquitaine, was ceded to the English by the Treaty of Brétigny, but the forces of the French king recaptured it later, and it became part of the front line between the opposing armies. The English held on to the castle at Castelnaud until the war ended in 1453, and the valley of the Dordogne became a constant battleground between the two armies.

It is an impressive building, with massive double perimeter walls and a crenellated keep defending it from the north. To the south the cliff falls sheer from the ramparts for nearly 170 metres to the river bank. The interior, too, is impressive, with a vast state hall where the lords of Périgord used to assemble.

From the ramparts there are stunning views of the valley, including Castelnaud and the Château de Fayrac, and extending as far as Domme. A circuitous road winds round behind the village to the castle as an alternative to the long steep climb from the valley. There are several hotels and restaurants in the village, as well as a number of shops and a museum of prehistory.

A short distance downstream, the Vézère joins the Dordogne on its way to the Atlantic. This, too, has a lovely valley, famous as the location of the caves of Lascaux at Montignac and those at Les Eyzies-de-Tayac, where you can visit the National Museum of Prehistory.

Between Les Eyzies and Montignac is the pretty riverside village of St-Léon-sur-Vézère. Near an old stone bridge close to the wooded river bank is a delightful Romanesque church and, in the village centre, an elegant château dating from the fifteenth century. A few kilometres upstream on the left bank is the Château de Losse, set romantically on a rocky bluff overlooking the river.

A short distance to the east of Montignac, hidden in the secluded wooded valley of the little River Coly, is the old village of St-Amand-de-Coly. Rising high above the rust-red rooftops is the massive arched façade of an ancient abbey church.

Monpazier

About 25km south-west of Beynac as the crow flies is Monpazier, one of the most charming and attractive of all French villages. It is one of a group of *bastides* built to defend the strategic route between the Dordogne and the Agenais. Construction began on 7 January 1264 on the orders of Edward I, Duke of Aquitaine and King of England, with the aid of his ally Pierre de Gontaut, the lord of Biron. However, political disagreements

delayed progress, and during the Hundred Years War the village was ransacked frequently by both English and French forces.

The village also played a role in the peasant uprising of the Croquants, which began in Limousin in 1593 after the end of the Religious Wars. They had held a huge gathering in Monpazier and, after a major outbreak of violence in 1637, one of their leaders was hunted and captured by the Duke of Epernon and taken to the village square, where he was broken on the wheel.

It is hard to imagine that such a picturesque and peaceful place could harbour such barbarous memories. It is surrounded by arcaded houses which date from the fourteenth century, and on one side is a covered market hall, with a roof supported on ancient timbers, still containing the old grain measures.

At one corner of the square is the church of St Dominique and nearby the thirteenth-century Maison de Chapitre, originally the tithe barn. The village retains the classic *bastide* grid pattern to a remarkable degree, and three of its original fortified gateways remain. There are several hotels and restaurants as well as a number of shops.

About 10km due north of Monpazier, overlooking the valley of the River Couze, is Montferrand-du-Périgord. In the company of such illustrious villages as Domme, Monpazier and Beynas, little Montferrand has tended to remain almost unknown. A steep narrow street climbs up from the valley floor to the ruins of a château at the summit of the hill. There is an ancient covered market hall, a church and many old houses and farms with turrets and *pigeonniers* hidden among apple and walnut trees. From the natural parapet upon which the castle is perched there are sweeping views over the surrounding countryside.

To the south-west of Monpazier are the *bastides* of Villeréal and, further south, Monflanquin, both founded by Alphonse de Poitiers in the thirteenth century. Monflanquin has an attractive arcaded square overlooked by a fifteenth-century fortified church.

The ancient square of Monpazier seen from the covered market hall that occupies one side.

AUVILLAR · COLOGNE
ST-BERTRAND-DE-COMMINGES · ARREAU

The Garonne is one of France's largest rivers, flowing from its source in the Spanish Pyrenees to its confluence with the Dordogne, where it forms the estuary of the Gironde, the river of Bordeaux. Along with its sister river, the Dordogne, it was an important navigable waterway for many centuries.

Auvillar

The wine producers of south-west France in particular thrived because of the international trade which these two rivers helped to create. The name of the region in between, Entre-deux-Mers, indicates that, for trading purposes, this strip of land, many miles from the Atlantic ocean, was effectively between two seas.

The village of Auvillar, about 30km south-east of Agen, began as one of the many ports which developed along the banks of the Garonne, and is mentioned in records going back to the ninth century. Its riverside location and fertile surroundings led to a steady increase in prosperity.

During the Albigensian crusades the village took the side of Simon de Montfort against the counts of Toulouse. Like most of the south-west of France, Auvillar suffered during the Hundred Years War, so much so that their feudal lord, the Count of Armagnac, exempted them from taxes. After the treaty of Brétigny, Auvillar, along with Armagnac and the Lomagne, remained under French rule.

During the Religious Wars the village, resolutely Catholic, was attacked by the Huguenots, and Auvillar was destroyed along with the feudal château. When peace was restored, the village rebuilt its prosperity under the influence of Louis XIV's finance minister, Colbert, and factories making pottery and writing quills were established.

The heart of the village is a beautiful

*The covered market hall of Auvillar and the
red-brick arcades which surround the square.*

square surrounded by elegant timber-framed houses and arcades built of red brick. In the centre of the square is a picturesque round market hall supported on stone columns which give it a curiously Tuscan appearance. It was reconstructed in 1828 in the original style, and its grain measures are still in place.

There is a fine gateway and clock tower of the same red brick construction, dating from the seventeenth century. The church of St Pierre is fourteenth-century, but was restored in the nineteenth. From the watch path there are fine views of the river and, below, the ancient port. There are many fifteenth-century houses, notably that of Bertrand de Goth, who later became Pope Clement V. It's a lively community with a number of shops, cafés and restaurants and a museum exhibiting the pottery for which the village became famous.

Down river from Auvillar, about 125km north-west via the E72 autoroute, is St Macaire, an atmospheric medieval village on the edge of the Landes, with well-preserved ramparts, towers and gateways dating from the twelfth century. Set on a rock between the river and vineyard-covered hillsides, it is a renowned wine village with its own appellation of Côtes de Bordeaux. The Place du Mercadieu is surrounded by ancient arcades and many old houses dating from the fifteenth and sixteenth centuries.

One of these, a post house in the time of Henry of Navarre, has been converted into the regional postal museum of Aquitaine. The church of St Sauveur has a terrace with a fine view of the Garonne. In the neighbouring town of Langon there is a good hotel, the Claude Darroze, which has an excellent restaurant.

To the north of Auvillar, between the Garonne and the Lot, is an attractive region of unspoilt countryside and quiet country lanes. The little village of Frespech is a

Old timber-framed houses surround the grand square in the bastide of Cologne.

sudden and delightful surprise, hidden away in a corner of the wooded hills south-east of Villeneuve-sur-Lot. It is a minute but perfect fortified village built of silver-grey stone, complete with a pretty Romanesque church, a château, ramparts and gateways.

To the north, set on a steep domed hill overlooking the Lot, is Penne-d'Agenais. It was a fief of the English kings during the Hundred Years War and was virtually destroyed during the Religious Wars. It is now a pleasant village which through careful restoration has managed to retain a distinctly medieval appearance and atmosphere.

There are two fortified gateways, including the Porte de Ricard, named after Richard the Lionheart, who first fortified the village. Here there is an ancient fountain. Along the strenuously steep paved streets, are many fine old timber-framed houses built of red brick, some of which are now art galleries and craft shops.

At the summit of the hill is a modern sanctuary built in Byzantine style which is the subject of an important pilgrimage between May and June. There is a superb view of the Lot reaching from Fumel to Villeneuve from the viewpoint nearby.

To the west of Penne-d'Agenais, on a hilltop overlooking Villeneuve-sur-Lot, is the medieval village of Pujols. The small walled village is entered through a tunnel under the bell tower of the church of St Nicholas, leading into a small square with a covered market where a market is held on Sunday mornings.

Although Pujols and Penne are only a few miles apart, Pujols is quite different, being built of granite instead of red brick. The narrow streets contain many old houses and the little village creates an appealing and evocative ensemble. On the edge of the village is a comfortable modern hotel, Les Chênes, and adjoining it is an excellent restaurant, La Toque Blanche, which has deservedly earned a *Michelin* rosette.

Cologne

South of the Garonne on the eastern border of Gascony, the landscape of folds and ridges begins to smooth itself towards the vast plain of Toulouse. Here, to the north of the N124 from Toulouse to Auch, lies the village of Cologne. It is a classic *bastide*, founded in 1286 by Odon de Terride and the French King, Philippe le Bel. Many of the *bastides* in this region, such as Granade, Fleurance and Barcelonne de Gers, were named after famous European cities, doubtless to add a touch of glamour to a new development and to attract potential residents.

The Gascons are especially proud of their squares, and while I was taking photographs in Cologne a young man came to watch and pass the time of day. He told me that the square of Cologne had been internationally acknowledged as one of the finest of its kind and was ranked, in its own category, alongside St Mark's and Place de la Concorde. It is an unusually spacious square, surrounded by arcades and some fine old timber-framed houses built of red brick. In the centre is a large market hall with a half-timbered centre topped by a bell tower.

To the south of Cologne, on the banks of the Arize, a small tributary of the Garonne, is the old village of Rieux-Volvestre. In 1317 Pope Jean XXII, who was a native of Cahors, made Rieux the seat of a bishop, and the village grew steadily in prosperity through the Middle Ages.

In the seventeenth century a new cathedral with a beautiful three-storey octagonal bell tower was built on to the old sanctuary

which rests beside a fifteenth-century bridge on the river bank. There are several fine old timbered brick houses with wrought-iron balconies and carved windows. On the first Sunday in May a colourful medieval festival is held, with a procession through the streets.

To the north-west of Cologne, off the road to Fleurance, in the Lomagne, is the large and attractive *bastide* of St-Clar. It is unusual because it has two squares, both surrounded by arcades. This arose as the result of an agreement in 1274 between the English King Edward I and the Bishop of Lectoure to build a *bastide* adjoining an existing village which had developed around a Benedictine church founded in the tenth century. It is named after St Clair, a martyr who was the first Bishop of Albi. In the centre of the village is the Place de la Mairie, with a covered market and the town hall. There are a number of shops, and the village is known for its garlic market.

St-Bertrand-de-Comminges

To the south-west of Rieux, in the upper valley of the Garonne, is St-Bertrand-de-Comminges, one of the great landmarks of the central Pyrenees: a Gothic cathedral of impressive proportions which can be seen from many miles away set on a hill below a wooded mountain range.

The village was founded in 72BC by Pompey, a Roman general returning with an army from a victorious campaign in Spain. The town prospered, accumulating a population of more than fifty thousand and earning the title 'The Rome of the Pyrenees'. It was important enough to be the place to which Herod was reputedly exiled after the crucifixion of Christ.

The cloister of St-Bertrand-de-Comminges.

In AD409 the Vandals destroyed the lower part of the town and the inhabitants were obliged to retreat to the higher level of the town within the walls. Remains of the Roman settlement can still be seen below the hill. Christianity arrived in the town around this time, and a church was built.

In AD585 the town was completely destroyed by Gontran, the King of Burgundy, and the site remained empty for five hundred years. In 1120 Bertrand de l'Isle, a member of one of the noble families of Gascony and a canon of Toulouse, had the vision to conceive the building of a great cathedral on the remarkable site and began a construction which took twenty years to complete.

The cathedral was enlarged and remodelled at the end of the thirteenth century by Bertrand de Goth, the future Pope Clement V. Only the cloister, the west tower and the porch remain from the earlier Romanesque period, and most of the existing building is from the later time. The village suffered during the Religious Wars but it was spared during the Revolution, although it was re-named Hauteville and its status as a diocese was removed.

A fortified gateway leads through the ramparts into a narrow street flanked by ancient houses. At the top a flight of steps lead up to the cathedral doorway which is surmounted by a twelfth-century tympanum. Inside are carved oak choir stalls commissioned in the sixteenth century by Bishop Jean de Mauléon and executed with great flourish and, often, macabre humour.

The greatest attraction of St-Bertrand, however, apart from its magnificent setting are the cloisters, which afford a superb view over the wooded mountainsides along the Garonne valley. There are many fine cloisters in this part of France, such as those at Moissac, but the tranquillity which is inherent in such places is enhanced enormously in those of St-Bertrand by their exhilarating mountain aspect.

Further up the valley is the ancient fortified village of St Béat, a row of grim granite houses strung out along the river bank in a gorge guarding the way to the Val de Aran and Spain, earning for it the title 'The Key to France'.

To the south-west of St-Bertrand is a region called the Barousse, through which the River Ourse follows a wooded valley. Flower-strewn meadows flank the fast-running river, and it makes a peaceful and relaxing spot for walks and picnics.

Arreau

To the west of St-Bertrand, carving a parallel course to the valley of the Garonne, is the Aure valley. It is part of a region known as the Four Valleys, along with the Barousse, Neste and Magnoac, which was an autonomous domain administered by the counts of Armagnac during the fourteenth and fifteenth

Arcaded houses overlook one of the two squares in the bastide of St Clar.

centuries. The former capital of this region, set at the confluence of the Aure and the Louron, is Arreau.

This is an attractive and lively place, with the sound of rushing water echoing along the narrow streets. In the summer it can be very busy, as it is set at the foot of two passes and lies on a main route through the Pyrenees to the tunnel of Bielsa, which leads into Spain.

There are many old timber-framed houses with steep slate roofs and wooden balconies. The Maison du Lys is an extraordinary building dating from the sixteenth century, its façade decorated with an elaborate pattern of carved wooden fleur-de-lis. Nearby, beside the river, is an old timbered market hall. The church of Ste Exupre dates from the thirteenth century and has a colonnaded Romanesque doorway. There are several hotels, cafés and restaurants in the village, and a number of good shops where regional specialities can be bought.

The village lies at the starting-point of the Col de Peyresourde, which leads to the valley of the Pique, and the Col d'Aspin, which leads to Bagnoles de Bigorre and the Pic du Midi de Bigorre. From here, at nearly 3,350 metres, there are stunning views of the Pyrenees.

An excellent short scenic circuit can be made through magnificent mountain scenery by following the small road from Ancizan, 6km south of Arreau, to Payolle and then returning to Arreau descending via the Col d'Aspin.

A feature of this region are the ancient communities known as *granges*, tiny villages of rough stone houses where the herdsmen tended their cattle. Many are isolated and can only be reached on foot, but the Granges de Lurgues, in an idyllic mountain valley, can be reached by a forest road which leads into the mountains from the village of Aulon, a few kilometres south-west of Ancizan.

The old market hall of Arreau.

FOURCÈS · BASSOUES
LABASTIDE-D'ARMAGNAC · AINHOA

Gascony is especially famous for two things, musketeers and Armagnac. During the seventeenth century many of the noble families of the region sent their sons to Paris, to join the royal army and make their fortunes. Charles de Batz, or d'Artagnan, was born near the village of Loupiac, where the family château can still be seen.

Fourcès

Armagnac was one of the ancient counties of the region, but its name has become synonymous with what many believe to be the finest distilled liquor in the world. The centre of the vineyard area, from which the brandy is produced, is the small town of Condom. It is in the heart of one of the most pleasing landscapes of south-west France, a countryside of big round hills which dip and rise in a series of grand ridges which reach away under a seemingly endless sky.

A few kilometres north-west of Condom, set on the banks of the River Auzoue, is the little *bastide* of *Fourcès*. Like many of its counterparts in the south-west, it was granted a charter by Edward I of England in 1289 and named after Guillaume de Fourcès, a son of the Count of Fézensac, a powerful feudal lord of the region. The family were loyal to the English crown, and in 1315 Bertrand de Fourcès supported Edward III in his campaign against Robert the Bruce. At the time of the war of St Sardos, a local dispute at the beginning of the Hundred Years War, the stronghold was dismantled on the instructions of Edward III.

The present château, built in around 1500, has corner towers and an attractive setting on the river bank beside a small stone bridge. The delight of Fourcès, however, is its central round square which is planted with plane trees and surrounded by old houses supported on both wooden and stone arcades.

The minute fortified village of Larressingle.

Little remains of its original walls, but there is a fortified gateway under a tower capped by a small belfry.

There are two café-restaurants, a *gîte* and a small museum of local history in the village. On the last Sunday in April a grand flower market is held under the plane trees in the small square.

A short distance to the south-west of Fourcès is Montréal-du-Gers, another larger *bastide* founded in 1285 by Alphonse de Poitiers. Set on a spur of rock overlooking the valley of the Azouze, it was one of the first *bastides* in Gascony built to guard the Aquitaine frontier. Much of the village was destroyed during the Revolution, but it has preserved a fortified gateway and sections of its ramparts. Some old arcaded houses remain around its square, and there is a fortified church set on the edge of the escarpment.

The village has two small hotels and a restaurant, together with a museum of Gallo-Roman remains discovered at the site of a villa at nearby Séviac. In August a *course landaise* is held in the village, a form of bullfighting in which the animal is not killed, merely tormented. The animal, partially tethered by ropes, is provoked into charging at its opponent, who stands his ground until the very last moment, often exiting by a dramatic somersault leap over the animal's back.

To the east of Montréal-du-Gers, surrounded by vineyards, is one of the smallest and most enchanting fortified villages in France, Larressingle. The village evolved around an eleventh-century church and was fortified in the middle of the thirteenth century when it came under the rule of English Gascony.

The ramparts, punctuated by watchtowers, are formed by the rear walls of houses built in a circle around the church and château, which was the residence of the

*A*ncient arcaded houses in the single street
of the small village of Tillac.

bishops of Condom. Once you have passed through a gateway in a large crenellated tower, it takes all of five minutes to walk round the narrow circular street, along which the old stone houses are fenced in by tree-like hollyhocks. There is a small café and a shop where you can buy regional specialities and the village's own brand of Armagnac.

Bassoues

To the south of Larressingle, beyond the market town of Vic-Fézensac, is the *bastide* of Bassoues on the D943 west of Auch. Local tradition claims that the origins of the town are linked to a knight called Fris, the son of the King of the Frisons and the nephew of Charles Martel, who was killed there in a victorious battle with the Saracens in the eighth century. Centuries later his perfectly preserved body, still in armour and with his sword by his side, was discovered under a rock by a local cowherd.

First a church was constructed on the site and later, in 1022, the Benedictines founded a monastery dedicated to St Fris. The *bastide* was built by the Archbishop of Auch, the feudal lord of Bassoues in 1279.

The village is quite small and, curiously, entered through a covered market hall straddling the main street which is bordered on each side by ancient half-timbered houses. At the far end of the street an incongruously tall tower soars above the rooftops. It is the keep of a château which was built in 1371 by the nephew of Pope Innocent VI, Archbishop Arnaud Aubert. There are splendid views from the top of the four-storey tower, and on a good day you can see the Pyrenees.

To the south of Bassoues is the minute village of Tillac. The single main street is guarded at each end by fortified gateways, and on either side stand rows of very old timbered houses supported on wooden arcades.

Labastide-d'Armagnac

To the west of Fourcès, on the edge of the great pine forest of the Landes, is the village of Labastide-d'Armagnac. It was founded in 1284 by Edward I of England and Bernard IV, Count of Armagnac. In spite of having been ransacked by the Catholics under the leadership of Monluc during the Religious Wars, it has remained one of the loveliest of all the *bastides*, on a par with Monpazier and Sauveterre-de-Rouergue.

The pride and joy of Labastide is its central square, Place Royale. It is a spacious square of pleasing proportions, surrounded by fine old houses and arcades which have been sensitively restored.

Here I was again reminded of the pride of Gascons concerning their squares. While taking photographs here, I was twice informed that the square was used as the model for Place des Vosges in Paris, which was also called Place Royale before the Revolution. There is a fifteenth-century church in one corner of the square and many attractive old houses in the streets leading off it. There is a small hotel-restaurant in the village, called L'Aubière.

Ainhoa

To the south-west of Gascony, beyond the vast forests of the Landes, is the Pays Basque, a region which extends into Spain, populated by a race who uphold their unique customs and language with fierce pride. It is a largely mountainous area, bordered by the Pyrenees to the south, the Atlantic to the west and the valley of the Ardour to the north.

The architecture in this region is very distinctive, reminiscent of that in Spanish

*A corner of the beautiful arcaded square
in Labastide d'Armagnac.*

Navarre. The village of Ainhoa, south of Biarritz, is one of the most typical and unspoiled of the villages. Set among green wooded mountains its tall, chalet-like houses with their brightly painted wooden balconies and rust-coloured tiled roofs create an almost fairy-tale scene.

The village was founded at the end of the twelfth century as a staging post on the pilgrim route to Santiago de Compostela. In the seventeenth century the village suffered a harrowing experience, when more than five hundred women were accused of witchcraft by Pierre de Lancre and they were dragged to

Characteristic Basque houses overlook the main street in the village of Ainhoa.

St-Pée-sur-Nivelle, where they were burned alive.

Ainhoa has several hotels and restaurants, and the region is dotted with many charming hotels. There are several in the neighbouring village of Sare, to the west, which is likewise very attractive, with many beautiful old houses and farms and a galleried church with

a gilded Baroque altar-piece on view.

Nearby Espelette, north-east of Ainhoa, is another lovely village, which is famous for the Pottoks, tiny horses which were at one time exported to England for work underground in the coal mines. Now they are used for a happier task, and along the roadsides you will see signs advertising 'promenades aux pottoks'.

To the north-east of Espelette, in the valley of the Joyeuse, is Labastide-Clairence, founded in 1314 by the Béarnaise. A steep main street climbing the hill is lined by arcades and galleried houses built of white stone and decorated with red-painted balconies and shutters.

To the north-east, the curious small *bastide* of Hastingues is set on a hill overlooking the River Gave d'Oléron. It is named after John Hastings, the seneschal of the Plantagenet King Edward I, who founded it in 1289. It has a fortified gateway, under a large tower, and a single street, lined by houses from the fifteenth and sixteenth centuries, leading to a charming little church square shaded by cypress trees.

Following the valley of the Gave d'Oléron upstream, one arrives at the pleasant old town of Sauveterre-de-Béarn, set on a bluff overlooking a bend in the river where the arch and tower of a ruined bridge jut out into the water.

About 40km south-west of Sauveterre is St-Jean-Pied-de-Port, a major staging post on the route to Santiago de Compostela, where the pilgrims prepared to cross the Pyrenees over the pass of Roncesvalles. It is very picturesque, but crowded in summer. Within its fifteenth-century walls many ancient houses line the narrow streets and the banks of the little River Nive, which rushes through the town.

CHAPTER SIX

SOUTH-EAST FRANCE

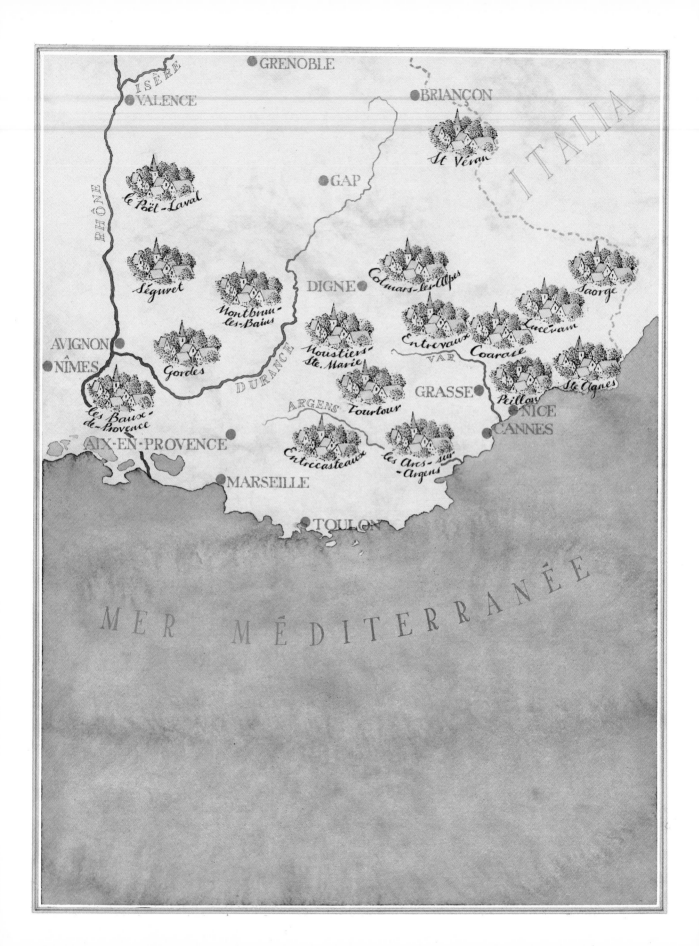

LE POËT-LAVAL · SÉGURET · MONTBRUN-LES-BAINS
GORDES · LES BAUX-DE-PROVENCE

The Rhône is not the most glamorous of rivers. For much of its length it is wide, turgid and industrialized, looking less like a river than a water-laden motorway. South of Lyons it shares its valley with the A6 autoroute, which millions of motorists use to speed them from Paris and the north to the sunny pleasures of the Mediterranean. To the east and west of the Rhône valley, within easy reach, is fine unspoiled countryside, of which many travellers remain unaware in their rush to reach their destinations as quickly as possible.

Le Poët-Laval

To the south of Valence on the east side of the river is one such neglected region, the Drôme. It is named, as most French *départements* are, after a river, which flows northwest from its source in the Dauphine to join the Rhône. Here one can enjoy the climate and light of Provence without the crowds and the fuss which the more southerly parts of the region attract. This is a land of wooded mountains, olive trees, vineyards, fields of lavender and undiscovered hilltop villages.

On a steep hillside in the valley of the Jabron is one of these villages, the curiously named Le Pöet-Laval. It lies either side of the D540, which runs east of Montélimar towards Dieulefit. The old village, north of the main road, is approached along a narrow winding road from the valley floor, and the ramparts are entered through a fortified gateway into streets only just wide enough for a car.

The village was established in the twelfth century by the Hospitallers of St John of Jerusalem, an order of warrior monks, as an important command post in the region, with a keep and defensive walls. When the Hospitallers were disbanded the village became a base for the Knights of Malta in the fifteenth century who renewed the defences.

The château and village houses of Le Poët-Laval. (Previous page) Looking westwards over the rooftops and vineyards of the village of Séguret.

The site was abandoned in the last century, but was made a protected monument in 1924. Since then many of the old houses along the narrow cobbled street which climbs the hill have been restored, some becoming art galleries and craft workshops. A comfortable and atmospheric hotel with a good restaurant, Les Hospitallers, has been created in the commander's residence. Another house has been turned into a museum devoted to the history of the Protestant religion in the Dauphine.

West of Le Poët-Laval is another fascinating hilltop village, Châteauneuf-de-Mazenc. It lies just to the north of La Bégude-de-Mazenc and has fine views over the valley of the Rhône from a lofty wooded hillside. Entered through a fortified gateway, the tiny village is threaded by narrow alleys and tunnels with many ancient houses. It has not been as extensively restored as Le Poët-Laval, but there is a small craft shop which sells locally-made pottery, fabrics, jewellery and metalwork.

About 20km south of La Bégude-de-Mazenc is the village of Grignan, dominated by a massive eleventh-century fortress. The village was made famous by Madame de Sévigné, a celebrated writer whose daughter was the Countess of Grignan. She was a frequent visitor to the village, and it was here that she died in 1696. Her tomb can be seen in the sixteenth-century collegiate church of St Sauveur.

To the north of Châteauneuf-de-Mazenc, a short distance from the Montéli-mar Nord exit of the A6, is Mirmande. This is a very pretty medieval village of grey stone houses covering a domed hill and surrounded by vineyards and orchards of peach and almond trees. It has been carefully and sensitively restored and is very much a lived-in village with a number of shops.

It also has an attractive hotel, La Capitelle, in a beautiful Renaissance building. From the twelfth-century church on top of the hill are splendid views of the Rhône valley and the mountains of the Vivarais. The village has been abandoned until a painter, André Lhote, established a small artists' colony here. Now it can provide a most agreeable, and convenient, overnight stop for those travelling on the motorway.

Séguret

To the south of Le Poët-Laval and due east of Orange is one of the most beautiful regions of Provence, Mont Ventoux, a wooded *massif* which rises to over 830 metres and is covered in conifers, holm oak and beech. In the hollows are fields of lavender, and on the slopes are some of the most celebrated vineyards of the Rhône, around villages with names that are familiar from wine labels.

It is here that the full red wines of Gigondas and Vaqueyras are produced, and the celebrated sweet white dessert wine of Beaumes-de-Venise. The importance of wine in this region is underlined by the presence of the university of wine, housed in the magnificent feudal castle which rises above the old rooftops of the village of Suze-la-Rousse. There is also a well-signposted *route des vins* which leads through some of the most attractive countryside and a succession of interesting villages.

One of these is *Séguret*, 9km south-west of Vaison-la-Romaine. The small village of grey stone houses and red-tiled roofs is set against a steep cliff-like outcrop of rock and looks out over a featureless plain to the west, patterned by endless rows of vines. The ruins of a fortress are set at the summit of the rock. The village has its own appellation of

Côtes-du-Rhône Villages, and there is a *cave co-opérative* where you can sample and buy the local wines.

Séguret is entered by a fortified gateway which leads into a tiny square with an ancient stone *lavoir* and fountain. A narrow street climbs the hill with splendid views over the red-ridged rooftops of the old houses. It is the sort of place which fulfils most people's image of a Provençal village, and it attracts many visitors.

A distinctive feature is the village belfry, which dates from the seventeenth century, and there is a ninth-century church and a thirteenth-century chapel to be seen, as well as remains of the ramparts. But it is the atmospheric location of Séguret and the charm of its old streets and houses which make it such a popular place. There are two hotel-restaurants, each with a reputation for excellent regional food, another reason for listing this delightful village.

To the south-east of Séguret are the Dentelles de Montmirail, a distinctive cock's-comb shaped mountain ridge on the western edge of Mont Ventoux which can be seen from many miles away. There is a fine scenic road, the D90, leading through the vineyards along the Dentelles from Beaumes-de-Venise to Malaucène. From here the D974 climbs to the summit of Mont Ventoux.

This region was an independent feudal domain known as the Comtat de Venaison, and its capital was Venasque, a small village to the south of Mont Ventoux. It has a spectacular setting on a lofty cliff-like bluff above the valley of the Nesque and contains some interesting old streets and buildings as well as a promising hotel.

Montbrun-les-Bains
Just north of Mont Ventoux is the deep narrow valley of the River Toulourenc. Perched giddily at its junction with the River Anary, with old houses tiered up the side of a steep hill, is the ancient village of Montbrun-les-Bains. Its name stems from the brown-tinged mountain which overlooks it and from a sulphurous spring which has been used therapeutically since Roman times for respiratory illnesses. The spring was abandoned at the beginning of this century, but its use has recently been revived.

The village and its domain were ruled by a succession of noble families until the beginning of the fourteenth century, when a certain Bastet Dupuy became the feudal lord. A descendant, Fouquet Dupuy, was the father of 32 children, one of whom, Aymard Dupuy, became a soldier of great renown, and was one of Louis XIII's commanders at the Battle of Naples. His son, Charles Dupuy-Montbrun, also became a famous soldier, with many heroic exploits to his name, but fell foul of Henry III during the Religious Wars and was beheaded in 1575.

The modern village is built at the foot of the hill and a small road climbs steeply up to

The old village and thermal spa of Montbrun-les-Bains.

the gateway which leads into the oldest part of the village where the narrow main street is dark and tunnel-like. Four towers of the castle remain, as well as sections of the ramparts, and there is a fourteenth-century belfry. The church contains a beautiful altarpiece carved in the seventeenth-century by Bernus. There is a hotel, a *pension* and a number of restaurants in the village. Nearby are distilleries for the lavender and herbs grown in the surrounding countryside.

A kilometre or so to the west of Montbrun, in a beautiful riverside setting, is the old village of Reilhanette, and further along the valley of the Toulourenc is the spectacular village of Brantes. Partially derelict, it harbours a number of artists. Orpierre, an old stone village 25km north-east of Montbrun, is also worth a visit.

About 25km to the south-east of Montbrun, set on a hill overlooking wooded hills and open farmland, is the ancient village of Simiane-la-Rotunde. It is a fascinating network of impossibly steep cobbled streets, steps and alley-ways with tall houses of rough stone soaring above. At the top is the building which gives the village its name, two-storey hexagonal tower which dates from the twelfth century.

To the east of Simiane-la-Rotunde, overlooking the valley of the Durance, is the medieval village of Lurs, its silver-grey houses covering a domed hill like icing on a bun. It was an important stronghold during the Middle Ages, with a population of more than three thousand. The community belonged to the bishops of Sisteron, who held the title of Princes of Lurs. It became deserted at the end of the last century and fell almost into ruins. The village was rediscovered by Maximillian Vox, the author of a classification of printers' typefaces, and slowly the village was restored and repopulated. It is now the location of an annual international conference of graphic artists.

The village is entered by a fortified gateway beneath a clock tower. Inside, the streets meander between ancient stone walls, which in the summer months are covered in flowers. There are two restaurants in the village.

Gordes

To the south of Mont Ventoux is the Plateau de Vaucluse and, further on, the Montagne du Lubéron. Between the two, set on a rock overlooking the valley of the Imergue, is the village of Gordes. It is the perfect Provençal village, with tiers of mellow stone houses rising from the plain like a multi-faceted sandcastle. At the summit is a Renaissance château and a church. The views from its terraced streets of the valley and the distant Lubéron are superb. Steep narrow streets and alleys paved with rough stones thread their way between many fine houses from the sixteenth and seventeenth centuries.

Gordes was once the home of noblemen, merchants and craftsmen, and a centre for tanning, silk weaving and cloth making. Many of the doorways and windows are finely decorated, reflecting its former wealth. After the eighteenth century the population diminished and the village fell into disuse. At the end of the Second World War it was almost in ruins. It was rediscovered, like many medieval villages in France, by artists, and has gradually been restored, some of the village houses becoming galleries and craft workshops.

There are several hotels and restaurants in or near the village, as well as *gîtes ruraux* and *chambres d'hôte*. The château houses a museum of the painter and sculptor Vasarely.

During the first week of July a cultural festival is held in the village, and there is a wine fair in the middle of July.

Just south-west of Gordes is the curious village of Les Bories, a community of igloo-like dwellings built of rough dry stones. It has been made into a museum of rural life.

The lofty village of Roussillon lies about 10km east of Gordes. It is a remarkable sight, for the houses are perched on the very brink of an ochre cliff which soars high above the plain. There are quarries in the area, from which the stone is extracted in colours ranging from pale yellow to a deep rust brown. The village houses are built of this stone, and in the evening sun, when the yellowing light is reflected from wall to wall,

the effect is stunning. Roussillon is a lively village, and much visited, with shops, cafés, restaurants and a number of hotels.

In the foothills of the Montagne du Lubéron to the south of Gordes is the old village of Ménerbes, stretched out along a rocky ridge. It is a site which has been occupied from ancient times and was a Roman settlement, its name stemming from Minerva, the Roman goddess. During the Religious Wars it was a Huguenot stronghold and one of the last to fall, holding out against a siege for five years before finally capitulating.

There are impressive remains of the citadel, with its towers and ramparts, as well as a twelfth-century church to be seen. Today

A street leading to the fortified entrance gate of Roussillon.

the village is partially deserted, and many of the houses are derelict, but it has an atmosphere which seems to recall something of its turbulent past. There is one hotel in the village and two restaurants.

A few kilometres to the east, in a striking setting on the slopes of the Lubéron, is the village of Bonnieux. There is a network of interesting old streets to explore, and from a terrace above the church there are sweeping views over the plain of Vaucluse. Unlike Menerbes, this is very much a live village, and has a number of good shops, hotels and restaurants.

On the southern slopes of the Lubéron, overlooking the valley of the Durance, is Ansouis, a mountain village with a fine Renaissance château which has belonged to the Sabron family for centuries. From its terrace you can see the distant heights of Mont Ste Victoire.

Les Baux-de-Provence

To the south-west of the Montagne du Lubéron the landscape flattens towards the Rhône delta. This is extremely fertile countryside, planted with vineyards, almond trees and orchards, and rows of tall poplars to shelter the crops from the ferocious blast of the mistral. In the midst of this plain, to the south of the city of Avignon, is a curious ridge of bleached rock. It makes an imposing sight and, from its heights, affords a dominating view of the surrounding countryside.

The view of Les Baux-de-Provence from the ancient ramparts of La Ville Morte. (Previous page) The hilltop village of Gordes lit by the setting sun.

Not surprisingly, this was for many centuries the site of a stronghold, known as Les Baux. The feudal lords of Les Baux, who included the notorious Raymond de Turenne, were among the most powerful of the region, controlling, and terrorizing, a large part of the south of France and threatening even the King. It was their custom to make prisoners, and unredeemed hostages, jump from the fearsome cliff on which the citadel was built. Ironically, the court of Les Baux was also famed for its troubadours and stories of love and romance.

During the Middle Ages, the population swelled to as many as six thousand. References to the lords of Les Baux begin as early as about 950 and end in the reign of Louis XIII, who finally dismantled the fortifications in 1633. The village revived during the nineteenth century with the discovery of aluminium ore, which became known as bauxite.

Although today the first impression of the village is that of a tourist trap, it still has an extraordinary atmosphere. The lower, newer village consists of a single street which climbs the hill and is lined with shops, boutiques, art galleries, cafés and restaurants.

Beyond, on the higher slopes of the ridge, is the *ville morte*, which was largely destroyed in the seventeenth century. It is here that you begin to sense the greatness which the place once had. As you climb to the highest point of the rock and walk along the remains of the walls, it is easy to see how the lords who lived here must have thought they would be impregnable for ever. The busy cafés and souvenir shops are only a few hundred metres below, but as the wind whips over the sun-bleached stone and you look across the sweeping plain you can imagine what it must have been like here when the lords of Les Baux were at the height of their power.

There are numerous hotels around the village. One which deserves special mention is the Oustau de Baumanière, an atmospheric former Provençal farmhouse on the outskirts of the village. The cuisine is outstanding, and dinner served on the terrace on a warm summer evening is a memorable event.

The food of Provence has a quality all of its own – aromatic, richly flavoured and full of the goodness of best basic ingredients. You only have to wander around a country market in this region and see the wonderful variety and quality of the produce (the Saturday market in neighbouring St Rémy-de-Provence is marvellous) to understand why the food here is so delicious.

Soupe au pistou is a dish which reflects these qualities admirably, a soup made with fresh summer vegetables which is enriched and flavoured with a paste made of garlic, basil, cheese and olive oil. *Boeuf en daube* makes similar use of vegetables, slowly cooked with chunks of beef, together with wine, oil and garlic, producing a distinctly Mediterranean flavoured version of the classic *boeuf bourguignon*.

The nearness of the Mediterranean also ensures fine seafood in Provence. *Bouillabaisse* is the famous soup-like stew of mixed fish simmered in oil, garlic and herbs, of which every restaurant has its own definitive version.

On a simpler level, the *pan bagna* makes a delicious casual lunch or snack, a sort of *salade niçoise* of vine-ripe tomatoes, tuna fish, anchovies and egg, liberally laced with fruity olive oil and wine vinegar, flavoured with garlic and basil and crammed into a large roll – wonderful with a glass of well-chilled rosé from the Côtes de Provence.

ST VÉRAN · COLMARS-LES-ALPES · ENTREVAUX
MOUSTIERS-STE-MARIE

ome of the highest and most exciting parts of the French Alps are surprisingly close to the Mediterranean beaches and the perfumed hills of Provence. The old frontier town of Briançon, for example, is only a hundred miles or so as the crow flies from the seaside resorts of Nice and Cannes. Dominated by a huge fort created by Louis XIV's architect, Vauban, Briançon is said to be the highest town in Europe and is the centre of some of France's most beautiful Alpine scenery.

The small valley of the Clarée which runs to the north of Briançon is a delight. The river, its clear water bubbling, flows between sloping meadows dotted with fir trees. A succession of small remote villages, including Plampinet and Névache, lie along this valley, with old stone houses covered with wood-tiled roofs which have changed little over the centuries. In these small mountain valleys, life is virtually self-supporting, with meat, eggs, milk, cereals and vegetables all produced in small plots on the valley floor.

To the north-west, the valley of the Guisane leads up to the Col du Lautaret, beyond which, in the valley of the Romanche, is the old village of La Grave, with the massive peak of La Meije towering above.

The River Durance flows south from Briançon, and a short distance to the north-west of L'Argentière-la-Bessée is the village of Vallouise, sheltering in the valley of the Gyr. Named in honour of Louis XI, the village has many fine old houses and farms with wooden balconies, as well as a fifteenth-century Gothic church.

Further down the Durance valley, near Guillestre is the curious fortified village of Mont-Dauphin on a promontory at the junction between the Durance and the Guil. Designed by Vauban in 1693 and built of pink marble, it is a complete city in miniature, contained by a rectangle of massive walls, and

The spectacular Château-Queyras as seen from the bridge over the River Guil.

took nearly a hundred years to complete. It is well preserved, with small craft workshops and exhibitions established among the old buildings, which include the officers' quarters, the powder store and the arsenal.

The valley of the River Guil leads up into what is, arguably, one of the most beautiful parts of the French Alps, the Parc Régional du Queyras. In the middle of the valley is Château-Queyras, an imposing fortress set on a spur where the mountain slopes meet almost in a 'V'. The castle has existed since the fourteenth century but has been altered several times, and until 1967 was occupied by the army.

St Véran

Beyond Château-Queyras the little D5 road leads south into the mountains to one of the most beautiful of the mountain villages, St Véran. It claims to be the highest village in Europe, although another village in Spain's Sierra Nevada make a similar claim. Such quibbling seems irrelevant, however, for its setting is breathtaking and quite superb.

St Véran is built high on the south-facing slope of the mountain, and in front of it is a breathtaking vista of peaks. Another claim is that it has over three hundred days of sunshine a year, which may well be because the village is usually above any clouds which may exist. St Véran was clearly built to glory in the sun, as all the houses are positioned so as to receive its light from sunrise to sunset, and the air here really does warrant the cliché: as clear and clean as spring water.

The village is equipped on a modest scale for skiing, with lifts and a number of hotels and restaurants, but in spite of this has managed to remain quite unspoiled. Because of the danger of fire, the village is divided into separate segments, each with its own holy

cross, bread oven and fountain. Many of the houses date from the seventeenth century, and one of these has been turned into a museum showing the traditional way of life in the region. The houses are very tall, built of stone, with two or three wooden balconies one above the other. Ancient wooden fountains bubble along the narrow streets which cling to the mountainside, and the outlook on all sides is stunning.

St Véran is named after a bishop of Cavaillon who was credited with slaying a ferocious dragon which had terrorized the area. A track from the village leads higher into the mountains, past a disused marble quarry, to a chapel, 2,400 metres up, to which there is an annual pilgrimage by both French and Italian devotees on 16 July.

Colmars-les-Alpes

To the south of the Queyras lies the Parc National du Mercantour, a protected mountain landscape rich in wildlife. Boar, ibex, moufflon, chamois and eagles can all be seen

A detail of one of the ancient wooden chalets in the mountain village of St Véran.

here if you are lucky. On the western edge of the mountains, in the upper valley of the River Verdon, is the old walled village of Colmars-les-Alpes. Its name is derived from a temple built in the narrow pass to the god Mars, but the village itself developed around a church which was erected on the site in the eighth century.

In the Middle Ages, when the upper valley of the Verdon was made part of the Duchy of Savoy, the village became an important frontier post and was fortified to defend the route through the mountains. Around this time the stronghold was burnt by Raymond de Turenne, one of the lords of Les Baux. In the early part of the sixteenth century, on the orders of François I, the fortifications were renewed and the ramparts

and towers which can be seen today were built, although they too have been damaged several times by fire. In 1690 the Duke of Savoy declared war on France and the village was unsuccessfully besieged. This, however, led to the addition of two forts which were constructed nearby under the direction of Vauban.

The walled village is entered through fortified gateways flanked by towers. Inside there is a delightful network of narrow streets, containing shops, cafés and restaurants, as well as three hotels.

Colmars makes an excellent base from which to explore the Mercantour and for the numerous walks in the area. A map is displayed near the tourist office, showing the signposted routes for ramblers. The Fort de

The walled village of Colmars-les-Alpes sheltering in the upper valley of the river Verdon.

Savoie is only a short distance away, on a hill to the north-east, and is well worth visiting.

There's a superb view of the village, and its dramatic mountain-flanked setting, from a small road which leads east from the village towards the Col des Champs. The Cascade de la Lance can be seen by taking a footpath which starts opposite the church and takes you along a narrow gorge.

The River Verdon is famed for its spectacular gorges downstream beyond Castellane, but the upper reaches are also very beautiful and can best be seen by following the riverside road, the D908 and D955, south from Colmars to St-André-les-Alpes.

Entrevaux

Some 10km or so downstream from Colmars the D908 climbs eastwards out of the Verdon valley and descends into the small valley of the River Vaire, at the head of which is the old village of Méailles strung out along an outcrop of limestone. The valley is shared by the railway line which runs from Digne to Nice, and from the station at Annot steam train journeys can be made to Puget-Théniers in the valley of the Var.

Annot is a very atmospheric old town with a grand square shaded by ancient plane trees and surrounded by cafés and restaurants. The old part of the town is a maze of narrow streets, steps, tunnels and alleys, lined by ancient houses, some of which are derelict. The sound of rushing water is everywhere as small streams from the mountains run alongside and under the streets.

From Annot the N202 runs eastwards down the valley of the Var to Entrevaux, a village built on the left bank of the river below a giant pyramid of rock, on top of which are the remains of a fort. The village was built in the eleventh century by the inhabitants of Glandeves, a Roman city which no longer exists. In 1690, during the war between France and Savoy, Louis XIV decided that the fortifications should be strengthened, and the prolific Vauban built the ramparts which you see today.

The village is entered over a drawbridge and through an impressive gateway, the Porte Royale, which is flanked by towers. There are two other gateways, the Porte de France and the Porte d'Italie. Tall houses from the seventeenth and eighteenth centuries make the narrow streets into deep dark tunnels. Near a large square is the cathedral, which was first built in the twelfth century by the Bishop of Glandeves, although the structure you see today is largely from the seventeenth century. The interior is richly furnished and decorated with a large gilded altar-piece and a fine eighteenth-century organ.

From the village a fortified path zigzags up to the citadel, from where there are stunning views of the Var valley. A fine view of the village, valley and citadel can also be obtained by taking the small road which leads

The fortified village of Entrevaux built to guard the valley of the Var.

up into the mountains to the south towards the Col de Félines. There are a number of shops and hotels in the village.

Moustiers-Ste-Marie

From Colmars the River Verdon flows south to St-André-les-Alpes, beyond which it enters the Lac de Castillon, which was created by a dam. On emerging from the lake, it continues through Castellane before entering its gorges. These are among the great sights of southern France, with a sequence of spell-binding views from the road which hugs the right bank of the river as it winds its way westwards towards the Lac de Ste Croix. A few kilometres to the north of the lake is the village of Moustiers-Ste-Marie, built below the face of a massive mountain of bare rock which is split in two by the valley of the small River Maire, a tributary of the Verdon.

Here an astonishing sight meets your eyes. A 225-metre chain is suspended across the chasm between the two mountains, and from it hangs a gilded star cross. The feat of suspending it was originally performed by a knight, honouring a grateful vow made on his safe return from the crusades. Discoveries made in caves near the village indicate that the site was occupied as much as twelve thousand years ago. In the fifth century a retreat was established here in the caves above the River Maire by St Maxim, a bishop of Riez, with monks from the Iles de Lérins, islands off the coast near Cannes.

The village is built on a series of narrow terraces which are linked by steep, narrow streets and steps. Alongside, the small river which bisects the village rushes down in a cascade. Beside the river is a twelfth-century church, which was an important place of pilgrimage during the Middle Ages, a fact which is remembered each September with a

festival. At the top of the village is the chapel of Notre Dame de Beauvoir, reached by a steep footpath. Those who make the climb are rewarded by a magnificent view of the village and the valley of the Maire. The chapel was first built in the fifth century, but was reconstructed in the twelfth century and again in the sixteenth.

Moustiers-Ste-Maire is a lively and popular place, and there are numerous shops, cafés and restaurants, together with a number of hotels. The village is famed for its distinctive blue-glazed pottery, said to have been first introduced by one of the monks who came from Faenza in Italy. The heyday of the Moustiers pottery was during the eighteenth century, when there were as many as a dozen craftsmen working in the village. Production died out at the end of that century but was revived in 1925. There is now a museum, near the church, which traces the history of the Moustiers pottery, and a festival of pottery is held on the Saturday before Easter.

On the left bank of the Grand Canyon du Verdon, in the valley of the River Jabron, is the old village of Trigance, where a three-star hotel has been installed in the eleventh-century castle with its four towers. Nearby is the Moulin des Soleils, an ancient water-mill and now a simple restaurant, where you can watch the flour being milled and the bread baked in the wood-fired oven.

About 12km south-east of Trigance, on a rocky hillside overlooking the plateau of Comps, is the ancient fortified village of Bargème. This is the highest village in the Var, and it has a gloriously remote and romantic air. A fortified gateway leads into a single small street which climbs between flower-flecked stone cottages to a beautiful eleventh-century church. The ruins of a castle overlook the village.

The village of Moustiers-Ste-Marie sheltering under the brooding mountains.

LES ARCS-SUR-ARGENS · COARAZE · LUCÉRAM
SAORGE

From Aix-en-Provence the A8 autoroute leads eastwards to Cannes, Nice and the Italian border. This stretch of road runs like an artery through the heartland of Provence, where the combination of sea, sun and mountains acts like a magnet to millions of tourists. In the summer months it can be almost impossibly crowded, and some of the qualities which many people like most about this corner of France have sadly been lost.

Les Arcs-sur-Argens

The area is especially rich in medieval villages in spectacular settings. As you drive along the motorway each turn of the road seems to reveal yet another. Many, however, are best seen from a distance, some of them, such as Gourdon, having been excessively restored, prettified and commercialized.

Les Arcs-sur-Argens is a busy and attractive little town close to the autoroute and the N7, about 10km south of Draguignan. It's an important wine town, and the surrounding countryside is covered with vineyards.

On a hill above the town, however, is the old village of Les Arcs. But for its square Saracen tower jutting up from the rooftops it would be easy to overlook it, but that would be to miss a place of considerable charm. A circuitous road leads up from the town through a gateway into a small square. From here steep cobbled lanes wind down the hill past old stone houses and small shaded squares. It has been carefully and sensitively restored but, apart from a small hotel-restaurant, there is no sign of commercialism. One senses that the villagers have tried to keep its existence to themselves.

The village was once a barony, the domain of the Villeneuve family. The many traces of its early history include the remains of the towers, ramparts and gateways, as well as the church of St Pierre, dating from the eleventh century, and the chapel of Ste

*A small manor house in the old village of
Les Arcs in the valley of the Argens.*

Rosaline from the same period. The village has an especially fine campanile which was made in 1662. This kind of cyndrical tower, with an iron-work cage containing the bell, is a distinctive feature of Provençal villages.

The castle was destroyed after the Revolution and all that remains of it is the Logis du Guetteur, a hotel with a restaurant set in the cave-like stone rooms of the tower.

To the north-east of Les Arcs, beyond Draguignan, there is a string of attractive old Provençal villages – Callas, Bargemon, Seillans, Fayence and Callian – all perched on the wooded mountainsides of the plateau of Comps. Another, to the east and slightly south of Callian, is the pretty, restored village of Auribeau, set on a knoll in the valley of the Siagne.

About 20km north-west of Les Arcs is the village of Entrecasteaux, sheltering in the valley of the River Bresque. High above the village is a severe-looking château built in the seventeenth century, with formal gardens designed by La Notre, the architect of the park of Versailles. The village is known for its Côtes de Provence wines and for its olive oil.

High on a rocky ridge north-east of Entrecasteaux is the delightful old village of Tourtour. Behind its gateways is a charming square, shaded by two huge elm trees which were planted in 1638. The church dates from the eleventh century, and among the picturesque old houses is an ancient oil mill.

At the edge of the village are the remains of two castles and a viewpoint from where on a good day you can see as far as the Lubéron to the west and the Massif des Maures to the south-east.

Coaraze

Inland from Nice, to the east of the Var valley, is a wild, mountainous landscape where there are a number of villages sheltering in the most startling settings. Although, as the crow flies, they are only short distances apart, the winding roads which link them climb up and around the mountains and take some time to negotiate, as well as providing breathtaking views.

Coaraze, known as 'the village in the sun', is set on a hill overlooking the valley of the Paillon de Contes, with a blue-grey mountain backdrop provided by the peak of Rocca Seira. There has been a village here for about a thousand years; the château was built around the beginning of the twelfth century, and the church in the thirteenth century. For centuries the village was passed back and forth between France, Savoy and the King of

Steep narrow streets and alleys tunnel between ancient houses in the village of Lucéram.

Sardinia, and it did not finally become French until after the Revolution.

The village seems like a honeycomb with its narrow passages, tunnels and steps, in which only pedestrians and animals were ever intended to travel. Only a three-dimensional model could fully illustrate the street plan of the village.

What was, in the Middle Ages, a thriving and influential community and the seat of a powerful feudal barony is now a peaceful and remote hideaway. A number of craftsmen and artists are installed in the village houses, some of which date back to the twelfth century, and there are cafés and restaurants. There is also a small hotel, the Auberge du Soleil, with rooms and a terrace affording splendid views over the Paillon valley. An olive festival is held in the village in the middle of August.

Lucéram

From Coaraze a small road leads north over the Col St-Roch, before dropping down to the ancient village of Lucéram, at the head of a small valley dominated by the peak of Gros Braus. The site was the capital of a region inhabited by a Ligurian tribe called the Lepontie. When the Romans arrived they made Lucéram a military post, and built fortifications which were later destroyed by the Moors. In the thirteenth century Lucéram, along with Peille and Utelle, became a small republic, but it was annexed to France in 1860 along with the comté of Nice.

Within the crenellated walls and towers, a warren of stepped lanes and alleys, with houses as early as fourteenth century on all sides, through which you climb towards the church. The latter was also built in the fourteenth century, but considerably altered in the eighteenth. Its treasures include many fine examples of religious art, notably altar-pieces by Louis Bréa, fourteenth-century silver and a sixteenth-century alabaster Virgin. The village has a Christmas festival, when the mountain shepherds bring offerings of lambs to the church in a procession accompanied by music from tambourines and pipes.

From Lucéram the road leads south to L'Escarène, where you can fork left to drive through the gorges of the River Paillon to the village of Peillon. The first glimpse is startling: against a background of the bare rock of the mountains you see the village on a crest of rock, on which its houses are tightly stacked, as if on an over-decorated cake.

The site was first inhabited by the Barbarians in the fifth century. Under the Emperor Charlemagne, Peillon became part of the comté of Nice and the kingdom of Provence. It was later made a dependency of the state of Sardinia, and did not become part of France until 1860.

Built of a silvery grey stone, the village is a gem, with passages, steps and alleys virtually tunnelled into the village. It has a twelfth-century church, a penitents' chapel with fifteenth-century frescoes, and, at the entrance to the village, a beautiful fountain which was built in the eighteenth century. Just outside the village, on the hillside, is an attractive hotel-restaurant, the Auberge de la Madone, with a panoramic terrace.

A short distance to the north of Peillon a looping road leads eastwards through the old town of Peille and over the Col de la Madone to the village of Ste Agnès. This too is a dramatically sited village with a backdrop of mountains and stunning views of Menton and the coast.

Ste Agnès has been skilfully restored, and has boutiques and galleries as well as a number of bars, restaurants and a small hotel.

But it has immense charm and has preserved a credible medieval ambience in spite of being rather trendy and very close to Menton. A film was being made while I was there, with a location crew at work and a pony-tailed director shouting instructions.

Saorge

From Menton another twisting road leads north over the Col de Castillon to Sospel and then crosses the Col de Brouis before it descends into the valley of the River Roya. Upstream the river runs parallel to the Italian border through steep-sided gorges. On the eastern side, high up on the cliff side and enclosed by a semicircle of rock, is the village of Saorge, in one of the most breathtakingly precarious settings of all Provençal villages.

From a distance it looks as if crampons and ropes will be needed to reach it, but in fact a gently sloping road leads up to it from

The village of Ste Agnès sits cradled in the mountains above Menton.

the village of Fontan, a little further up-stream. Saorge is completely unspoiled, being, I suspect, too far from the coast and Menton to attract many commuters or tourists. It is strongly Italian in both appearance and character, with mellow ochre-washed houses built on a series of narrow terraces and linked by steps and tunnel-like lanes.

The old church of St Sauveur was built in the fifteenth century and restored in 1718. The organ came by boat from Genoa and was then carried by mule train from Nice up the valley to Saorge. The church also contains a fifteenth-century font, a marble tabernacle installed in 1539, and a Virgin and Child sculpted in 1708.

At the southern edge of the village is a Franciscan convent, built in the seventeenth century, which has a cloister decorated with paintings. Further along the mountainside is the Madone del Poggio, a sanctuary established by the monks of Lérins in the twelfth century, where there is a soaring seven-storey Lombardy bell tower and a lovely seventeenth-century altar-piece.

A short distance to the north-east, in the valley of the River Levense, is the curious old village of La Brigue, where the ruins of the castle of the Lascaris can be seen. The old houses, many of them over stone arcades, are built of a green-tinged schist and decorated with heraldic crests. The fourteenth-century church has a fine collection of paintings and altar-pieces.

A few kilometres further up the valley, surrounded by springs and streams, is the pilgrimage chapel of Notre Dame des Fontaines, which contains frescoes from the fifteenth century. The river valley and surrounding mountains are very beautiful, and the village makes a good base for walks and excursions into the mountains.

The village of Saorge perches above the gorges of the River Roya.

CHAPTER SEVEN
SOUTHERN FRANCE

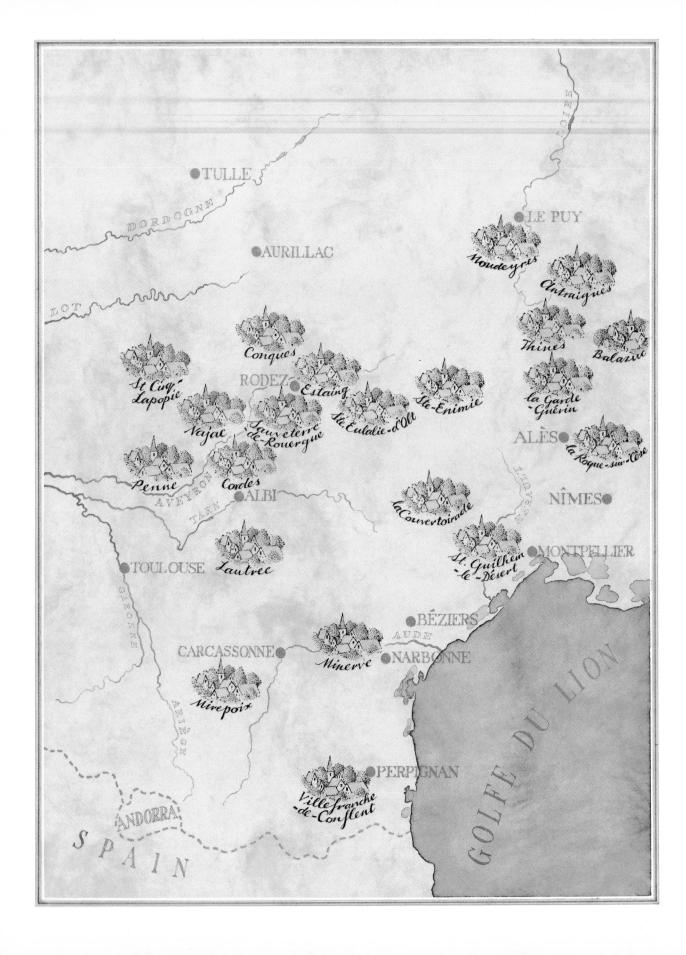

TULLE

DORDOGNE

LOIRE

LE PUY

Moudeyres

AURILLAC

LOT

Antraigues

Conques

Thines

Balazuc

St Cirq Lapopie

RODEZ

Estaing

Ste-Enimie

la Garde -Guérin

Najac

Sauveterre -de-Rouergue

Ste-Eulalie-d'Olt

ALÈS

la Roque-sur-Cèze

Penne

Cordes

AVEYRON

TARN

ALBI

la Couvertoirade

NÎMES

MONTPELLIER

Lautrec

TOULOUSE

St. Guilhem -le -Désert

GARONNE

BÉZIERS

CARCASSONNE

Minerve

AUDE

NARBONNE

Mirepoix

ARIÈGE

GOLFE DU LION

PERPIGNAN

Villefranche -de-Conflent

ANDORRA

SPAIN

BALAZUC · ANTRAIGUES · MOUDEYRES
LA ROQUE-SUR-CÈZE · THINES · LA GARDE-GUÉRIN

The Ardèche is one of France's loveliest water-ways, a grand, fast-running mountain river, its white-stoned bed carving a sinuous course through a magnificent landscape. Its source, in the north of the Cevennes, lies hidden in the Forêt de Mazan below the summit of Mont Mézenc at the watershed of the Massif Central. A short distance to the west, the Lot and Tarn head off towards the Atlantic, but the Ardèche flows in the opposite direction to join the Rhône on its way to the Mediterranean.

Balazuc

At first the river flows eastwards through cliffs and orchard valleys and then turns south to Aubenas. From here it runs through the countryside of the Vivarais before entering spectacular gorges and finally flowing into the swollen Rhône north of Pont-St-Esprit.

The Vivarais is a gentle, sheltered area full of vines and orchards, hidden between the hills which rise from the west bank of the Rhône and the foothills of Mont Lozère.

Balazuc lies in the heart of this countryside on the east bank of the Ardèche. It is built on the brink of a steep rampart-like cliff at a point where the river snakes through a tight gorge. A bridge crosses to the west bank, and a narrow road winds up the side of the gorge through a rocky, shrub-covered landscape dotted with small terraced vineyards.

From this road, the village and the silvery Ardèche make a memorable sight. Grey limestone houses are grouped around a fourteenth-century Roman church and surrounded by the remains of ramparts dating from the tenth century. The Saracens occupied the site during the eighth and ninth centuries, and during the Middle Ages it was an important stronghold for the silver-mine lords of neighbouring Largentière.

The village has no hotel but there is a

A street in the ancient robber stronghold of La Garde-Guérin. (Previous page) A distant view of the medieval village Balazuc set on a cliff above the River Ardèche.

restaurant, Le Buron, and there are a number of *gîtes ruraux* in the vicinity. During the summer, exhibitions and concerts are held periodically in the church. The nearest hotels are to be found in Largentière and Vogue, a pleasing village with an impressive château on the banks of the Ardèche.

Regional specialities include the red, white and rosé wines of the Côtes de Vivarais, a velvet-skinned goat cheese called Pelardon, a creamy blue cheese made from cow's milk called Fourme d'Ardèche, and *caillettes Ardèchois*. These are delicious sausage-like balls made from minced pork, herbs and finely chopped *blette* (Swiss chard), which are wrapped in caul fat and slowly fried.

There are probably more unspoiled medieval villages in this part of the Ardèche than anywhere else in France. A few kilometres to the south-west is Labeaume, in a very attractive setting on the banks of the River Beaume shortly before it joins the Ardèche. Further upstream the Beaume runs through beautiful gorges. The ancient village of Rochecolombe lies in an isolated spot east of, and close to, Balazuc at the head of a small valley.

Near Les Vans, to the south-west of Balazuc, is Naves, a village of rough stone houses and cobbled alleys which can have changed little during the past few centuries. A few kilometres south-east of Naves, near the hilltop village of Banne, is a curious landscape of stunted trees and outcrops of rock eroded into strange sculptured shapes. A similar landscape, called the Bois de Païolive, extends to the east of Les Vans.

In the remote and lovely valley of the Ibie, between Villeneuve-de-Berg and Vallon-Pont-d'Arc, is Les Salelles, a settlement of traditional stone farmhouses with distinctive covered balconies. Further east are the villages of St-Montant and St-Thomé, both in delightful settings with old houses threaded by stone-paved streets and tunnel-like alley-ways.

Another pair of historic villages are within easy reach of the town of Le Teil. To the north, set below a castle-crowned hill overlooking the banks of the Rhône, is the old village of Rochemaure, an impressive landmark in the valley, visible from miles away. North-west of Le Teil, about 9km away, is Aubignas, a delightful village built of limestone and volcanic rock and set at the head of a quiet valley. Undisturbed by the twentieth century, it has an impressive eleventh-century fortified church, well-preserved ramparts as well as an old vaulted entrance gate.

Antraigues

To the north of Vals-les-Bains in the upper valley of the Ardèche is the dramatic volcanic landscape of the Cevennes Ardèchois. It is in these mountains, dominated by the peaks of Mont Gerbier de Jonc and Mont Mézenc, that the great River Loire rises, over 950km from its estuary.

From Vals-les-Bains a road follows the valley of the River Volane north to the village of Antraigues, set on a hill at the point where the Volane is joined by the Mas and the Bise. It lies between two volcanoes, Craux and Aizac, in a landscape of steep rounded hills covered with forests. It dates from the sixteenth century and was the birthplace of the de Launay family, the counts of Antraigues. The château, overlooking the square, is still owned by the family, although apparently the present count lives in London.

There is a restaurant in the village square, La Montagne, which also has simple rooms, and there are several restaurants,

which include La Brasucade and Lo Podello in the square, where the menus contain regional specialities: the mountain charcuterie is especially good. In the valley below is the Hôtel l'Oeil de Boeuf, with a terrace overlooking the river.

This is exhilarating countryside with wonderful views and, in the springtime, the meadows are bathed in colour by drifts of wild flowers. Some of the most spectacular scenery of the region can be seen by following the valley road up to Mézilhac and then heading back south-east, over the Col des Quatre Vios (four winds pass), to the Col de Escrinet on the main road to the west of Privas. Alternatively you can take the Col de la Fayolle via the village of Genestelle back to Antraigues, of which you get a superb view from this road.

Moudeyres

The main road from Privas, the N102, leads west along the valley of the Ardèche to Pradelles, an attractive old village with an arcaded square which has a distinctly Spanish appearance. From here the N88 leads north towards Le Puy. At Costaros a road leads eastwards into the mountains to the tiny fortified village of Arlempdes, set beside the river Loire in its upper valley. The ruins of a twelfth-century castle are perched on the summit of a large rock overlooking a particularly beautiful stretch of the river. The Hôtel du Manoir shelters under the castle walls.

To the north-east, beyond Le Monastier-sur-Gazeille, is the small village of Moudeyres. It is a community of beautiful stone cottages and farms with steep thatched roofs peculiar to the countryside of the Velay.

The mountain village of Antraigues overlooking the valley of the River Volane.

One of the farms, La Ferme des Frères Perrel, has been converted into a museum with a faithfully restored interior showing the traditional way of life in this remote landscape. It is open from 1 July to 15 September every day except Wednesday. Near the small church, the Auberge des Chaumières has *chambre d'hôte* accommodation and there is a delightful and atmospheric hotel Le Prés Bossu, in a restored thatched manor on the edge of the village.

The speciality of this region are the round green lentils of Le Puy; like miniature peas they are delicious simmered in stock until tender and then tossed in butter with garlic and parsley.

A short distance to the north is Bigorre, another delightful hamlet of thatched houses built on the terraced side of a quiet hillside. It can be found by taking the road towards Le Puy from the village of St-Front. After a kilometre or so there is a small road off to the right signposted to Maziaux and Les Chaumières de Bigorre. One of the cottages has been made into an Eco-Museum and is open daily, except Wednesdays, from 1 July to 1 September.

La Roque-sur-Cèze

The most spectacular part of the Ardèche is to be found to the east of Vallon-Pont-d'Arc, where the river winds like a viper through deep wooded gorges towards the Rhône. To the south, another river, the Cèze, runs a parallel course. More modest but equally captivating, the Cèze also passes through gorges before crossing a fertile plain to join the Rhône south-west of Bagnols-sur-Cèze. Downstream from the gorges, and close to the Cascade de Sautedet, where the river descends a series of wide rock shelves, is the village of La Roque-sur-Cèze.

Thatched stone cottages, typical of the remoter parts of the Cevennes, in the village of Bigorre.

It is built on a small rounded hill and surrounded by vineyards. Rough stone-paved streets and steps climb to a Romanesque chapel and the remains of a castle. The village has been sensitively restored and is untouched by tourism. There are two small cafés in the village, and nearby, close to the river, are two restaurants.

A few kilometres to the north, built along a steep rocky ridge, is the wine village of Cornillon. From the remains of the ramparts there are sweeping views over the vineyards of the southern Rhône. There is a small auberge in the village. The neighbouring villages of St-Michel-d'Euzet and St-Laurent-de-Carnols are also known for their wines. A few kilometres to the north-east, hidden in a peaceful wooded valley, is the Chartreuse de Valbonne. Founded in the twelfth century and reconstructed in the seventeenth, the monastery has a beautifully decorated interior with a large cloister.

Thines

From the Ardèche plateau a number of river valleys lead up into the Cevennes towards Mont Lozère. From Les Vans, a winding road follows the valley of the River Chassezac along a wooded hillside. After 12km another small valley leads north towards Thines.

The narrow road climbs higher into the mountains and, far below, a river races over boulders. This is chestnut country, and in October the road is strewn with bulging burrs filled with glossy brown nuts. It is a remote, peaceful place, and the village is set high on a hill in glorious isolation at the end of the steep rocky valley. My first attempt to visit Thines was thwarted by a large boulder which had fallen on to the road; during the winter months it can be cut off from the outside world for weeks at a time.

The road ends at the village and within it rough tracks lead over rocks to a small community of crude stone houses tiled with the schist from the mountainsides. Thines was a staging post for pilgrims travelling from Le Puy to Santiago de Compostela and, in striking contrast to the severity of the village houses and its setting, there is a very pretty Roman church decorated with red and white stone. The nave is especially beautiful and the portal has four finely carved statues. A tiny flower-decked graveyard is next to the church serving a population that can seldom have exceeded double figures.

The only concession to visitors is a small café in the village where *tarte au châtaigne* (chestnut tart) is the speciality.

La Garde-Guérin

The road continues to climb the valley of the Chassezac eastwards until it emerges on to the lower slopes of Mont Lozère. Here, a few kilometres north of Villefort and overlooking the Chassezac ravine, is the fortified village of La Garde-Guérin. It can be seen from a long way off, marked by a soaring granite tower rising up from the rocky escarpment upon which the small village is built.

The Romans had established a trading route, known as the Regordane, connecting the Mediterranean ports of Languedoc to the Auvergne, and the village was originally a fortress built to defend it. Between the tenth and twelfth centuries it became a den of robbers and highwaymen who took passing travellers hostage and held them to ransom. The Bishop of Mende solved the problem by giving the bandits official status and allowing them to charge a toll for the protection of those whom they had previously robbed. Now the occupants are mainly farmers raising cattle and sheep on the village pastures.

The village of La Roque-sur-Cèze with its rough cobbled streets.

STE ENIMIE · STE-EULALIE-D'OLT · ESTAING
CONQUES · ST-CIRQ-LAPOPIE

The River Tarn rises in the wild desolate landscape of Mont Lozère, nearly 1,670 metres above sea level, and flows down to Le Pont-de-Montvert, the first village on its course. From here the road follows the course of the young Tarn through a wild and beautiful valley all the way to Ste Enimie, a small village situated at the entrance to the spectacular gorges for which the river is famous.

Ste Enimie

Ste Enimie is in a beautiful setting beside a bend in the silvery river as it races through a narrow, curving valley between the soaring mountainsides of the Causse de Méjean and the Causse de Sauveterre, which dwarf the village. There is a splendid view of it from the road which ascends the Causse de Sauveterre towards Mende.

It is an ancient community with a web of steep narrow streets behind the riverside promenade. The village was named after a legendary princess of the sixth century. The daughter of a Merovingian king, she contracted leprosy and was travelling to the spa of Bagnols-les-Bains in search of a cure. As she passed through the Tarn gorges with her entourage, she stopped to drink from a spring which emptied itself into the river, and almost immediately the disease began to leave her.

Soon she was completely cured and started the return journey to her home. The moment she emerged from the gorges, however, the disease returned. This happened several times, and she finally decided to remain in the valley, where she founded a small abbey, the remains of which are still to be seen in the village.

The fountain of Burle, said to be the miraculous spring, can be seen on the edge of the village near the road which leads up on to the Causse. There is also a twelfth-century Roman church, in which a modern ceramic

The château and old houses of Estaing rise above the banks of the River Lot. (Opposite) An old village house in Ste-Eulalie-d'Olt set in the upper valley of the River Lot.

panel illustrates the legend, and a hermitage chapel dating from the tenth century. There is a small museum of local history housed in an ancient building called Le Vieux Logis.

Ste Enimie has numerous hotels and restaurants, but the season is short and in early spring and autumn many of them are closed. A memorable place to stay is at the Château de la Caze, a fifteenth-century castle on the bank of the Tarn with an authentic medieval atmosphere.

A kilometre or so up river, on the left bank, is the tiny village of Castelbouc, set under a huge rock with the ruins of a castle above. The name means castle of the billy goat and is said to stem from the time of the crusades, when the lord of the castle was the only man left in the village and was called upon to exercise his seigneurial rights rather more than usual. Upon his demise – premature perhaps – his spirit is said to have taken the form of a huge goat. On the left bank, a few kilometres downstream from Ste Enimie, is the pretty little village of Chely-du-Tarn, set under a steep curving cliff.

Ste-Eulalie-d'Olt

From Ste Enimie, one road crosses the Causse de Sauveterre towards Mende and another leads north-west to the upper valley of the River Lot. After the dramatic gorges of the Tarn and the wild remote landscape of the Causse, the countryside of the Lot seems gentle and unassuming. Here the river flows quietly through wooded valleys between water-meadows where cattle graze and wild flowers fill the hedgerows.

In the heart of this countryside, on the left bank of the river, about 25km west of La Canourgue, is the mellow stone village of Ste-Eulalie-d'Olt. Dating from the twelfth century, the village was the home of many of

the nobility of the region, and had as its feudal lord the judge of the court of the Bishop of Rodez. In the seventeenth century the village had a number of tanneries and clothmakers, and along the main street are many large houses dating from this period.

The village church, a mixture of Roman and Gothic, dates from between the eleventh and sixteenth centuries and is a small-scale replica of the abbey church of Conques. There are two small châteaux and a working water-mill spanning a stream which flows into the Lot. This has been converted into an appealing little hotel-restaurant, Le Moulin d'Alexandre. The village also has another hotel and two restaurants.

On the second Sunday in July there is a festival and procession in which the villagers dress in period costume to represent the ascent of Jesus to the hill of Calvary. This has been a tradition for many centuries and celebrates the two thorns preserved in the church which, legend has it, are from Christ's crown. They were brought from the Holy Land when the feudal lord returned from the Seventh Crusade.

A kilometre or so upstream is the atmospheric old town of St-Geniez-d'Olt, which is renowned for its strawberries. About 20km downstream is the ancient fortified village of St-Côme-d'Olt, named after a hospice built on the pilgrim route to Santiago de Compostela. It retains sections of its ramparts and houses dating from the fifteenth and sixteenth centuries. Two towers remain from a fourteenth-century castle as well as two fortified gateways, a sixteenth-century church and a penitents' chapel from the eleventh century.

Estaing

About 20km down river from St-Côme-d'Olt is Estaing, one of the prettiest riverside villages in France. It is set on a bend just above the point where the Lot enters its gorges. Seen from across the river it presents an immensely satisfying view. A row of old houses runs parallel to the river bank and the village rises up behind, surmounted by a large fifteenth-century feudal château and ancient turreted houses. Behind the village is a green wooded hill ridged by terraced vineyards.

An old stone bridge spans the river and is decorated by a statue of François d'Estaing, once its feudal lord. He was a bishop at Rodez cathedral and was responsible for the construction of its magnificent bell tower. William I of Estaing was a companion of Richard the Lionheart, whom he met at the time of the Third Crusade. The village name derives from *estanh*, the laugue d'oc word for pond.

There are a jumble of narrow streets within the village which are crossed by ancient stone bridges and linked by flights of steps leading to the church and the château. Among the small shops is an excellent charcuterie and boulangerie for picnic supplies, and one which sells home-made regional preserves.

There are two hotel-restaurants, the Hôtel Reynaldy and Aux Armes d'Estaing, both with simple but comfortable one-star accommodation. The latter is situated by the old bridge facing the river. There are also two restaurants, Au Bel Horizon and Le Paradou.

Local specialities include *cou d'oie farcie*, a delicious sausage-like pâté made with chopped goose meat, pork and liver. *Tripous* is a similar sausage-like concoction but made with tripe and braised in a wine-rich sauce until soft and tender. There are vineyards on the steep surrounding hillsides, and Estaing has its own *vin de pays* appellation.

The village is the subject of a *son et lumière* presentation between 14 June and 6 September. There is festival on the first Sunday in July when the villagers go in procession to celebrate their patron, St Fleuret.

The countryside to the south-west of the village is a delightful region of wooded valleys, swirling rivers and cascades, with ancient red-stone farmhouses and small villages. Villecomtal, Muret-le-Château and Salles-la-Source are particularly appealing.

Conques

Down river from Estaing the Lot emerges from its gorges and flows through the attractive old town of Entraygues. Beyond the village of Viellevie the Lot is joined by the Dourdou, which runs through a steep wooded valley. High on the hillside, at the point where the river enters its gorges, is the village of Conques. This old village is

The village of Conques is dominated by the abbey church of Ste Foy.

unashamedly pretty, its golden stone houses with steeply pitched, brown-tiled roofs ranged in rows up the hillside on a series of shallow terraces linked by narrow zigzag lanes and steps.

Views of the village, however, are dominated by the soaring structure of a magnificent abbey church set on a broad terrace overlooking the rocky valley. It took a hundred years to build and was completed in the middle of the twelfth century.

Why such a small isolated village should have such a large and imposing church is explained by a flagrant and carefully-planned act of theft. In the ninth century Conques was the site of a small abbey on the pilgrim route to Santiago de Compostela. Both abbey and village were immensely poor, and the abbot devised a plan. One of his monks entered the rich abbey at Agen, which housed the relics of Ste Foy, a child-saint responsible for miraculous cures. After ten years of faithful service the monk was given the post of guarding the valued relics. One dark night he simply stole them and, aided by his miraculous booty, escaped his pursuers and carried them to the abbey of Conques.

The story does not end there, however. The grand new abbey, built by the wealth created by the stolen relics, fell into disuse when, in later centuries, the previously vast number of pilgrims making the journey to Spain dwindled to a trickle. It still possessed its relics, however, together with the treasures amassed during its period of affluence.

During the Revolution many of the treasures owned by abbeys and churches all over France were seized by the Republicans to raise funds. The mayor of Conques was determined to save theirs, so he distributed the contents of the abbey's treasures among the villagers on the understanding that when things settled down they would be returned to the church. And so today the abbey still contains one of the finest collections of medieval treasures in France.

There are four hotels in the village, of which the Hôtel Ste Foy, opposite the abbey, is particularly good, and five restaurants. The village stages concerts during July and August and in August there is a *son et lumière* presentation at the abbey. There is a pilgrimage procession on the second Sunday in October.

There are two superb vantage-points from which to view the village and abbey. One is from the small road which climbs up behind the village towards Noailhac. The other is from the opposite side of the valley at the Site du Bancaral. This can be reached by a small road which leads up from the valley road, the D981, in the direction of Marcillac.

St-Cirq-Lapopie

From its confluence with the Dourdou near Conques, the River Lot flows past Decazeville and Capdenac before entering one of its most attractive stretches on its way to Cahors. Between Pont-de-la-Madeleine and St-Géry it runs through a series of faults in the limestone *causses*, and much of the valley is bordered by ochre-tinged cliffs. There is a succession of small villages and castles along its course – St Pierre-Toirac, Larroque-Toirac, Cajarc, Salvagnac and Cénevières – and the route is a constant pleasure. Just before the Lot is joined by the River Célé, the village of St-Cirq-Lapopie comes into view on the south bank, perched high on the side of a steep cliff overlooking a curve in the river.

Like Conques, it is quite spectacular. The mellow stone, timber-framed houses are built in tiers up the hillside, their steep roofs,

wooden balconies and small towers creating a picturesque geometric pattern. In Gallo-Roman times the village was called Pompejac, but in 701 St Amadour brought the relics of a third-century saint, St Cyr (the q is silent in Cirq), to the village, and a feudal lord named La Popie, who built a castle here in the tenth century, gave it its present name.

The ruins still look down from the crest of the rock above the village. The castle saw a great deal of action through the centuries, thwarting Richard the Lionheart but changing hands several times during the Hundred Years War. In 1580, during the Religious Wars, the Huguenots under Henry of Navarre finally took the castle and demolished it.

The village was known for its wood-turning skills since the time of Louis XI, and during the nineteenth and early twentieth centuries it was a major producer of the wooden taps fitted to wine casks.

Some of the houses date from the thirteenth to the sixteenth century; one, known as La Gardette, housed the feudal lord when he was obliged to vacate his castle. It is now a museum. The great Gothic church is fortified and dates from the late fifteenth century.

There are three hotels in the village and four bar-restaurants. I can recommend the Hôtel de la Pelissaria, a sensitive conversion of an old village house with a small terraced garden, from where there are grand views of the river and village.

The valley of the little River Célé contains a number of attractive villages, such as Cabrerets, Marcilhac-sur-Célé and Brengue. Espagnac-Ste-Eulalie is an especially charming small village of typical turreted Quercynois farmhouses with dovecots. It has a picturesque thirteenth-century priory church.

Looking down over the old rooftops of St-Cirq-Lapopie towards the River Lot.

NAJAC · SAUVETERRE-DE-ROUERGUE
CORDES · LAUTREC

outh of the Lot valley the River
Aveyron follows a winding route
through the poor rye-growing countryside known as the Ségala. For much of
its course it is inaccessible by road,
passing through small isolated valleys and
rocky gorges. To the south of Villefranche-
de-Rouergue, on the border between Quercy
and Rouergue, it enters a twisting and tor-
tuous gorge which is surrounded by steep
wooded hills. Here, set on a rocky spur above
a bend in the river, is the fortified village of
Najac.

Najac

It is an impressive sight, with the substantial
remains of a castle perched high up at one
end of the village, and the houses strung out
below it along the ridge. From a distance it
looks every inch the imposing medieval
stronghold it once was.

An earlier castle stood on the site, built
by Bertrand de St-Gilles, the son of Raymond
IV, Count of Toulouse, who established the
village as the administrative centre of the
Rouergue. In the early thirteenth century this
castle was destroyed by Simon de Montfort
during his crusades against the Cathars. In
1249 it was rebuilt by Alphonse de Poitiers, to
become a military garrison with a population
of over two thousand.

The Gothic church was built around this
time, paid for by fines levied on the defeated
heretics by Simon de Montfort's inquisitors.
It contains a number of wood and
polychrome statues from the fifteenth and
sixteenth centuries.

Many of the old village houses, built to
house the garrison's soldiers, are supported
on crude stone pillars. There are two ancient
fountains, one of which has a basin cut from a
huge block of granite, a coat of arms and the
date 1344 inscribed upon it.

There are two hotel-restaurants in Najac:

The arcaded square of Sauveterre-de-Rouergue.

the Bellerive, set in the valley beside the Aveyron, and the Oustal de Barry, overlooking the village square. An excellent local dish (on the menu of both restaurants during my visits) is *astet najaçois*, a fillet of pork stuffed with garlic, butter and parsley and baked in its own juices. The wine-growing region of Gaillac is a short distance to the south; the wines produced are predominantly red, but there is also a dry white called Gaillac Perle.

The old *bastide* of Villefranche-de-Rouergue to the north has a great deal of charm, with its arcaded square, good shops and a church with an immense tower. It was founded by Alphonse de Poitiers and has superb carved oak choir stalls by André Sulpice.

Sauveterre-de-Rouergue

To the south-east of Villefranche-de-Rouergue is a pocket of countryside known as the 'land of a hundred valleys'. The River Viaur runs through the centre of this region, which is threaded by numerous small rivers and streams. The old village of Sauveterre-de-Rouergue lies by the River Vayre in the midst of this peaceful and secretive landscape.

It is a *bastide* founded in 1281 by Guillaume de Macon, the seneschal of Rouergue. In 1330 the Bishop of Rodez founded a church here. The village developed quickly and was soon a centre of trade and commerce.

One of the best preserved of all the *bastides*, it has a particularly fine central square with an ancient well in the centre surrounded by arcades and many beautiful timber-framed houses. The deep tunnel-like arcades in mellow stone were built in the fourteenth and fifteenth centuries. The church contains choir stalls and a retable dating from the sixteenth and seventeenth.

There are two hotel-restaurants in the village, the Auberge du Sénéchal and A la Grappe d'Or. There is also a small regional

The minute castellated village of Brousse-le-Château sits on a spur beside the River Tarn.

museum and an exhibition of paintings, sculptures and tapestries, as well as a number of good shops. In October there is a festival of chestnuts and cider, with tastings and folklore displays.

A few minutes' drive away, in a small wooded valley to the south-east, is an appealing château hotel, the Château de Castelpers, set in a park beside a trout river.

About 40km further south-east is the curious little village of Brousse-le-Château, perched on a domed hill overlooking the River Tarn at its junction with the Alrance. It has the remains of a fortress, a fortified church, a pretty Gothic bridge and houses from the seventeenth and eighteenth centuries. The village is minute, with a series of small footpaths and steps linking the houses, among which are a number of artists' and craft workshops. There is a hotel, Le Relays de Chasteau, which belongs to the Logis et Auberges de France network, on the edge of the village beside the river.

Cordes

About 30km due south of Najac is the hilltop village of Cordes, overlooking a smiling landscape of woods and meadows in the valley of the River Cerou. This fortified village, dubbed 'Cordes in the Sky', was founded in the early thirteenth century to protect the inhabitants of the region against Simon de Montfort's crusaders. Occupying a naturally strong defensive position, and circled by several rings of defensive walls, it was never destroyed.

During the following century Cordes became a retreat of the lords of Languedoc, who built Italian-styled houses from where they would hunt in the surrounding countryside. In later centuries it became a flourishing commercial community, its prosperity based

Set on a steep hill the château and houses of Najac overlook the River Aveyron.

on the tanning of leather and the weaving of linen and hemp. The village suffered, however, during the Religious Wars, was virtually annihilated by the plague, suffered again during the Revolution and eventually fell into neglect.

In the 1940s the partially derelict village was discovered by a painter, Yves Brayer, who created a small community of artists. The old houses were gradually restored and soon the village became a tourist attraction.

One ring of ramparts is still largely intact and the village is entered by its imposing fortified gateways which lead into the steep cobbled Grande Rue. Here some of the grander houses can be seen, notably the House of the Great Falconer, now the town hall, and nearby the House of the Huntsman, decorated by sculptures of the chase. The former hunting residence of Raymond VII, one of the counts of Toulouse, is now a luxurious hotel with an excellent cuisine, the Hôtel le Grand Ecuyer. Many of the old village houses are now art galleries and craft workshops.

The church dates from the thirteenth century but was much altered in the nineteenth with the addition of wall paintings echoing those in the cathedral at Albi. The view over the valley of the Cerou from the original tower, a look-out post from earlier times, is well worth the climb.

There are numerous hotels and restaurants in the village, but it is an extremely popular place in the summer months and it is advisable to make a reservation. There is a medieval costume festival on 14 July and a music festival during July and August. A collection of Yves Brayer's paintings are displayed in the House of the Great Falconer, and there is also a museum of archaeology and local history.

To the west of Cordes, in the valley of the Aveyron, is Bruniquel, a fortified village perched on a rocky hill. It is surmounted by the ruins of a large castle overlooking the river and the Forêt de Grésigne. It is named after Brunhilda, a daughter of the King of the Visigoths, who lived here in an earlier fortress. There are precipitous views of the valley from the walls, and the village below has a tangle of interesting old streets.

A few kilometres upstream from Bruniquel is the extraordinary village of Penne. The ancient village, clustered around a tall pinnacle of rock, is surmounted by a ruined château which soars up from its overhanging sides like a rocket about to be launched. The village has its own *son et lumière* presentation during July and August.

Further up the river is St-Antonin-Noble-Val, a small spa. It has a Romanesque town hall built in the twelfth century, but 'modernized' by Viollet-le-duc in the last century, and there are houses dating from the thirteenth century.

To the south-west of Cordes, on the far side of the Forêt de Grésigne, is the ancient hilltop village of Puycelci. This village, founded in the twelfth century, was a possession of the counts of Toulouse. Now partially deserted, Puycelci has many houses from the fifteenth and sixteenth centuries, and a fifteenth-century château, towers and ramparts, from which there are superb views over the valley of the Vère and the Montauban plain.

About 12km south-east of Puycelci is another charming hilltop village, Castelnau-de-Montmirail, with an attractive and well-restored central square surrounded by arcaded timber-framed houses.

Lautrec

On a hill to the south-east of the village

Castelnau-de-Montmirail, and due south of Albi, beyond the vineyards of Gaillac, is Lautrec. It was built in the twelfth century by the counts of Lautrec, a family from which the great painter Henri de Toulouse-Lautrec was descended. Once it was a fortified village, but only one gateway now remains from this period, Le Port de la Caussade. The château, long since gone, was set on a hill to the west of the village. It is now the site of the Calvaire de la Salette and affords a fine view over the old rooftops to the Montagne de Noire and the Monts de Lacaune beyond.

The church of St Rémy was built in the fifteenth century and has a beautiful marble retable and lectern. The square is surrounded by arcades and timber-framed houses, and in the town hall is a museum of archaeology and local history.

Today the village is the centre of the production of pink garlic, which many connoisseurs believe to be the best. A garlic festival is held in August. There are no hotels in the village, but there are three restaurants.

Lautrec with its church spire and old rooftops.

LA COUVERTOIRADE · ST-GUILHEM-LE-DÉSERT
MINERVE · MIREPOIX · VILLEFRANCHE-DE-CONFLENT

The landscape of the Tarn region is dominated by the great *causses*. These are vast limestone plateaux, rising to over 1,000 metres, which are divided by rifts through which the rivers flow. They can be wild and desolate places, rocky moorlands with little habitation and no industry apart from the raising of sheep. The largest and most southerly of these, bordering the mountains of Haut Languedoc, is the Causse du Lazarc.

La Couvertoirade

In the most remote part of this rocky wilderness is the village of La Couvertoirade. Its unlikely presence is due to the fact that one of the pilgrim routes to Santiago de Compostela crossed the Causse between Millau and Lodève. The stream of travellers in the Middle Ages made rich pickings for the robbers and rogues who lay in wait for them along this isolated and exposed road. In 1158 the Prince of Aragon gave Lazarc to the Knights Templars, who established a pilgrim hospital at La Couvertoirade. When they were disbanded in 1311, it came under the control of the Knights of St John, who turned it into a miniature fortified city offering full protection to the pilgrims.

Although now largely deserted, and partially derelict, it remains very much as it was, with thirteenth-century houses, a Romanesque church, towers, gateways and ramparts, from which a precarious walkway provides vertiginous views of the Causse. Outside the village is a stone-lined dew-pond which was used to water the flocks of sheep.

There is a hotel, as well as several cafés and restaurants, and a number of artists and craftsmen are installed in some of the village houses. During the summer months there is an audio-visual display describing the history of the village, together with exhibitions, concerts and a *son et lumière* presentation.

*The tiny square of the industrial village
of Villeneuvette.*

St-Guilhem-le-Désert

To the south of the Causse de Lazarc is the valley of the River Hérault, which passes through beautiful gorges to the north-east of Clermont-l'Hérault. Here, on the right bank of the river, tucked into a cleft in the gorge, is the village of St-Guilhem-le-Désert.

The village was founded by Guilhem, a young knight in Charlemagne's service whose exploits became the subject of an epic poem sung by the minstrels of the Middle Ages. He defeated the Saracen king who was holding Orange and much of Languedoc, married his queen and seized his lands. In doing so he became Prince of Orange, founding what was to become the royal house of the Netherlands, whose sons are traditionally called William.

As an old man he became a religious recluse and lived in a hermitage in this remote rocky ravine. After his death he was declared a saint. An abbey founded in the valley soon became a place of pilgrimage and a staging post on the route to Santiago de Compostela.

The ruins of a castle on the crag above the village are said to have belonged to a Saracen who terrorized the region. Guilhem killed him in battle after having the tip of his nose cut off, giving him the nickname of Courtnez. Another version of his story claims that this happened while fighting with a giant on a pilgrimage to Rome.

The abbey, consecrated in 1076, contains a relic said to be a piece of Christ's cross given to Guilhem by Charlemagne. This is carried in procession each year on 3 May. Of the abbey's cloister only two arches remain; the others are now exhibited in New York's Metropolitan Museum.

A single narrow street lined by medieval houses leads uphill from the river bank to a small square which is shaded by a huge plane tree. There are also a number of shops,

The ancient village of St-Guilhem-le-Désert built in the gorges of the River Herault.

café-restaurants and additionally two hotels.

To the south of St-Guilhem, on the edge of the *garrigue*, is the grotto of Clamouse, a series of caverns containing spectacular stalactites and stalagmites. About 40km east of St-Guilhem, near the D986, lies the miniature medieval village of Les Matelles, complete with ramparts, fortified gateways and narrow winding streets linked by steps and tunnels. A few kilometres to the west of Clermont-l'Hérault is Villeneuvette. This small community was an industrial 'new town' created in the seventeenth century by Colbert, Louis XIV's minister of finance. It was established to weave the cloth used to make uniforms for the army. The village is entered through an imposing gateway which opens into a pleasing square shaded by chestnut

The walled village of Minerve with the gorges of the River Cesse below.

About 50km west of Clermont-l'Hérault on the D908 road is the old village of Olargues, set dramatically on a promontory in a bend of the Jaur with a thirteenth-century bridge spanning the river. Shortly before Olargues, a road leads south into the valley of the Orb. Here the little wine village of Vieussan, perched on the mountainside, overlooks a beautiful landscape pattenred with vineyards.

Minerve

To the south-west of Vieussan, about 40km as the crow flies, the River Cesse winds through a ravine in the rocky, mountainous landscape of the Minervois. In the heart of the canyon, on a natural promontory created by the confluence with the River Briant, is the walled village of Minerve.

The Midi is haunted by the memory of Simon de Montfort and his ruthless suppression of the Cathars. During the Albigensian crusades, many villages and towns in the region fell to de Montfort's sieges, and extraordinary acts of cruelty were carried out as punishment in the name of Catholicism. But the story of Minerve is especially tragic.

It is a village with a considerable history. The Romans settled here in the first century; in the fifth century it was a stronghold of the Visigoths, and in the eighth the Moors had a fortress in this spot. At the beginning of the thirteenth century the village was one of the last remaining pockets of Cathar resistance and Simon de Montfort came here with an army of seven thousand men, determined to take it. In June 1210 he began a siege which lasted for seven weeks. Deprived of water, the remaining 180 villagers surrendered and were offered the choice of conversion to Catholicism or death. They were all burned alive in a huge fire at the foot of the castle.

trees, under which an old, stone fountain plays. A number of artists' studios, craft workshops and shops now occupy some of the factory buildings and workers' houses; there is also a hotel-restaurant.

Further west lies the old village of Mourèze, set in the landscape of the Cirque de Mourèze, where lofty outcrops of rock are eroded into curious shapes and formations.

The village has many old houses, together with walls and gateways from the thirteenth century. The castle ruins also date from this period, while the church of St Etienne is two hundred years older. There is a museum of archaeology and pre-history and a small hotel-restaurant. Below the village walls are Les Pont Naturels, two deep tunnels created by a change in the river's course.

This is wine-growing country, and the valley is filled with the vineyards from which the hearty red Minervois wines are produced. In the village of Lézignan-Corbières, 30km or so to the south, there is a museum of wine, with exhibits explaining the history of wine production in the Languedoc. There is also an opportunity to taste and buy wines, regional foods and local crafts.

About 20km south-west of Lézignan-Corbières, on the banks of the River Orbieu, is the medieval village of Lagrasse. It is a *bastide* ringed by ramparts which were built at the beginning of the Hundred Years War around an abbey founded in the eighth century. Once known for its weaving, dying and tanning industries, it is now a centre of Corbières wine production.

Mirepoix

About 100km due west of Lagrasse, between the plain of Toulouse and the Arriège, is the medieval village of Mirepoix. There are records of the community going back to the tenth century. In 1209, during the Albigensian crusades, Simon de Montfort took the castle and gave it to one of his knights, Guy de Levis.

He became the lord of a small kingdom, and a village was built at the foot of the castle on the right bank of the River Hers. In 1279 there was a catastrophe – a dam burst, the river flooded and the small village was destroyed. The Levis family decided to rebuild it in the style of the period – as a *bastide* – on the other side of the river. In the fourteenth century four fortified gateways were added to protect the prosperous village from pillagers. One of these still exists.

Mirepoix is a classic *bastide*, built on strict geometric lines with streets criss-crossing in a grid pattern. The large central square is entirely surrounded by houses supported on slender wooden arcades, giving it a rather Spanish appearance. Many of the houses are decorated by wooden carvings; the consul's house is the finest example. It was originally the house of justice of the feudal lords and became the consul's house in 1500.

In 1317 Pope Jean XXII made the village the diocese of a bishop, and the small church was no longer adequate. The building of the cathedral was begun at the end of the thirteenth century but was stopped and restarted many times over a period of two hundred years. It has an impressive bell tower, over sixty metres high, and the largest nave to be found in a Gothic cathedral anywhere in France.

Mirepoix is a lively and attractive village with several hotels, cafés and restaurants.

The old church of Eus sits high above the village overlooking the River Tet.

There are good shops and a large covered market hall of wrought iron in which a market is held on Thursdays and Saturdays. A cattle market is held on the second and fourth Monday of each month. During the second fortnight in July the square is decorated and becomes the centre of a grand medieval fair in which the villagers dress up in costumes.

About 13km south-east of Mirepoix is Camon, a small village built around a Benedictine abbey which was founded in 923. The village was destroyed twice, in 1279 and 1494, and was reconstructed and fortified at the beginning of the sixteenth century. There are remains of ramparts and old houses dating from this period, together with a museum of religious objects, as well as exhibitions of paintings and tapestries. There is no hotel but there are three restaurants.

Villefranche-de-Conflent

To the south of Mirepoix are the foothills of the Pyrenees, a natural barrier between France and Spain which provides some of the most spectacular mountain scenery to be found in either country. In the eastern Pyrenees the Massif du Canigou dominates the landscape; visible from a great distance, it soars to nearly 3,000 metres. Below the peak is the valley of the River Tet, and at its junction with the Cady, north-west of the Canigou, the fortress-like moated village of Villefranche-de-Conflent stands purposefully astride the valley floor.

It was built in 1092 by Guilhem Ramon as the capital of the region and became one of the main border defences between France and Spain. In the region of Louis XVI the fortifications were extended by Vauban, who added massive walls, towers and fortified gateways. Inside is a complete village of dark narrow streets lined by medieval houses.

The church of St Jacques, built partly of the pink marble for which the region is known, is as old as the village itself, and was added to over the next two hundred years. It contains a fourteenth-century Virgin and Child. The village has two hotels, a restaurant, shops, cafés and a number of exhibitions. To the north of the village is a fortified bridge spanning the Tet.

In a pretty valley to the south-east, in the shadow of the Canigou, is Vernet-les-Bains, a small spa popular with the English and frequented by Anthony Trollope and Rudyard Kipling, among others. From here, motorized excursions can be made into the mountains and to visit the eleventh-century abbey of St Martin.

The valley of the Tet is filled with peach orchards, and the vine-covered hillsides are dotted with ancient villages. About 10km north-east of Villefranche is Eus, one of the oldest and most attractive of the hill villages. It is built on a series of narrow terraces, with slanting narrow lanes paved with stone threading between the old houses, the roof of one building level with the foundations of another. At the summit of the village is a large church built in the early eighteenth century. There is also a small Roman chapel dating from the eleventh century. The village has a hotel and a restaurant.

About 12km west of Villefranche, near Thuir, is Castelnou. This too is a dramatically sited village, surrounded by vine-covered mountainsides and with the Massif de Canigou looming above. Inside a fortified gateway, steep cobbled streets zigzag between rough stone houses, and a medieval castle is perched on the summit. It is a very pretty village and has been sensitively restored. There are a number of craft shops, small art galleries and a restaurant.

The impressive village of Salers (overleaf), nestling on a plateau of volcanic rock (see page 100).

INDEX

ACKNOWLEDGEMENTS

I would particularly like to thank Colin Webb for making it
possible for me to spend many happy months exploring a
country I love. Pat, my wife, I thank for holding the fort
and keeping the Indians at bay while I detoured to yet one
more mark on my Michelin map. I am also very grateful for the
benefit of Louise Simpson's and Andrew Barron's considerable
editorial and design talents in bringing it all to fruition.
I would also like to thank, posthumously, Freda White for
introducing me to some hitherto unknown villages and for
providing some fascinating historical anecdotes.
The photographs were all taken on a Mamiya 645 Camera
using Fuji RFP 50 film.
Thank you, too, to P&O European Ferries for their generosity in
helping me to cross the channel with comfort and ease many times.